Recognizing the Moment to Play
Anticipation - Imagination - Awareness.

by Wayne Harrison, B.A. , UEFA "A"

REEDSWAIN *Publishing*

**Library of Congress
Cataloging - in - Publication Data**

by Wayne Harrison B.A, UEFA "A"
    Recognizing the Moment to Play
    Anticipation - Imagination - Awareness

ISBN No. 1-890946-72-9
Lib. of Congress Catalog No.
2001098187

Editor
Bryan R. Beaver

Printed by
DATA REPRODUCTIONS
Auburn, Michigan

Reedswain Publishing
612 Pughtown Road
Spring City, PA 19475
800.331.5191
www.reedswain.com
info@reedswain.com

Contents

LEGEND FOR DIAGRAMS

⚽   Ball

┈┈┈┈►   Passing of the ball

───────►   Movement of the player without the ball

━━━━►   Movement of the player with the ball

②   Numbers Team

Ⓒ   Letters Team

Ⓚ   Keeper

Ⓒ   Coach

⌐‾‾‾¬   Small Goals

━━━━   Shape of Numbers Team

─────   Shape of Letters Team

INTRODUCTION

This Soccer Coaching Manual is presented to help understand the thought processes that a player goes through in playing this wonderful game of soccer.

It includes many practices the coach can use to reinforce what we are trying to establish in the players.

I have tried to introduce a new approach to soccer coaching that allows the players to develop their skills in a non-competitive environment to begin building up to working more competitively when the players are ready to progress to that stage. Initially each exercise should be practiced without opposition building up to exercises with opposition to test the composure the players should have gained by following the program.

Once the coach has covered all the aspects of the coaching exercises presented in the manual, he can keep the training of the players fresh by using different exercises at different times. But always he should have the same results in mind : to develop composure in possession of the ball, to increase time on the ball by anticipating situations ahead of time or decrease the time needed to move the ball by having total awareness of the positions of all players. He should encourage players to use their imagination in their use of the ball and allow them to make their own decisions.

Each chapter covers methods of coaching with built in progressions that compliment this learning program, beginning with the most basic introductory exercises to enable players to get an easy understanding of how to gain success in their application.

As each chapter is covered, the coach and the players can see that the exercises become more detailed in their content and that they encourage both the coach and the players to explore more difficult pathways providing further coaching plans to enhance their development as coaches and players.

By using the exercises provided the players' decision making will improve and the speed of those decisions will increase.

To begin to apply these ideas into game situations, later in the book you will find progressions involving the small sided game concept, beginning

ANTICIPATION, IMAGINATION, AWARENESS

with a 3 v 3 game situation through 4 v 4, 5 v 5, 6 v 6, 8 v 8, and ultimately touched on 11 v 11.

Success is specific to the ability of the player and the amount of work and effort the player puts in . This is an ongoing self - fulfilling process that any given player must continue to explore. It is not a program that a player practices then moves on , it must be a program that the player includes in all his future practices indefinitely.

The players must be both psychologically and physically prepared to meet the demands of the program. The process is ongoing throughout their playing career and will be further influenced by the experience gained from every coaching session and every game played over time. We are trying to establish the following in the players make-up:

A.   **WHAT** they do.
B.   **WHERE** they do it.
C.   **WHEN** they do it.
D.   **HOW** they do it.
E.   **WHY** they do it.

OVERVIEW OF THE A.I.A. PROGRAM

A.I.A - RECOGNIZING THE MOMENT TO PLAY

AN ANTICIPATION / IMAGINATION / AWARENESS YOUTH SOCCER COACHING PROGRAM

A PSYCHOLOGICAL APPROACH TO SOCCER

This system of coaching will begin to teach each player the psychological, physical, technical and tactical fundamentals of soccer and together these form the basis of the requirements needed to be able to play soccer. The degree of improvement a player attains using these aspects depends on his own commitment (in terms of repetition of practice and belief in the system) and level of ability. Don't expect results overnight. Players have to be patient in learning this new approach as it takes time and great concentration to develop.

The players must be both psychologically and physically prepared to meet the demands of the program. The process is ongoing throughout their playing career and will be further influenced by the experience gained from every coaching session and every game played over time. We are trying to establish the following:

1. **Using Correct Technique** to perform the task efficiently and effectively. Particular attention must be paid to the first touch of the ball by the players.

2. **Psychologically** being able to develop composure on the ball, to relax under pressure, creating in the mind of the player Imagination / Insight in the use of the ball; each pass is unique   to that moment.

3. **Tactical considerations** will be covered teaching the ability to look Beyond the ball, having the capacity to Anticipate Situations, an Awareness of others positions (own players, opponents and the ball) movements off the ball and an appreciation of Space.

4. **Physical work** will be a natural part of the program aiding relevant types of fitness.

5. The program is aiming to develop the above in all players to aid the **DECISION-MAKING PROCESS**.

THE DECISION MAKING PROCESS

1. OBSERVING HOW AND WHERE THE BALL IS COMING FROM.

2. KNOWING WHERE TEAMMATES ARE.

3. KNOWING WHERE THE OPPOSING PLAYERS ARE.

4. DECIDING " WHAT " TO DO WITH THE BALL. (TECHNIQUE / SKILL TO USE (EMPHASIS ON A GOOD FIRST TOUCH) - PASS, RUN, SHOOT, CROSS, DRIBBLE, DUMMY / LEAVE)

5. OBSERVING " WHERE " THE BALL IS TO BE MOVED OR PASSED TO. (WHAT ARE THE OPTIONS?).

6. DECIDING " WHEN " THE BALL GOES. (TIMING OF THE TECHNIQUE / SKILL USED).

7. DECIDING " HOW " THE BALL GOES. (TECHNIQUE / SKILL TO BE USED)

8. DECIDING " WHY " THE BALL GOES. (THE TACTICAL OBJECTIVE).

ANTICIPATION, IMAGINATION, AWARENESS

1. We as coaches are trying to coach players to establish 1) to 5) in their minds **BEFORE** they receive the ball (Anticipation) **NOT after**. Decisions of 6), 7) and 8) can be determined depending on how much time on the ball the player has. If he has no time and is being closed down as he receives it, he may have to determine these three aspects before receiving the ball as well. Otherwise, with time on the ball he can wait for the right moment depending on the positions of his team-mates and the opposition. This is when reaction plays a part in the process. The movement of the players constantly creates new situations on the field of play for the player on the ball to assess and respond to with the correct pass, dribble, run, shot, cross and so on.

2. The development of this system of coaching sets the foundations for the above process to be integrated into the players' make - up. It develops **QUICK DECISION MAKING** to allow them to work ahead of the opposition.

3. The sessions are designed to teach players to develop ability on the ball (developing a good first touch is the beginning) and ability to look beyond the ball (Awareness), i.e. **TECHNICAL** and **TACTICAL** ability.

4. The practices we use are **NO opposition** games to begin (SHADOW PLAYS), to allow a developmental program to take place without a loss of possession through pressurizing from defenders. Essentially there are no defenders, just other players who effectively simulate pressurizing situations by working in the same area. Using these methods of coaching we are giving the player a chance to develop **COMPOSURE** on the ball.

5. From the no opposition games we will introduce opposition, initially using an overload situation. Ultimately the coaching will include full scale practices to put players in the pressure situations they face on the field in regular team play.

6. This system of coaching is a long-term approach to improvement. Results don't happen overnight. We are creating a New Learning Environment for the player. The four aspects of work; Psychological anticipation, Technical ability, Tactical awareness and Physical capacity are inter - linked.

7. While a player has eight individual thought processes to consider, all these cannot be established in one go. Over a period of time the coach must try to increase the number of observations the player makes starting with number one; observing where the ball is coming from, this is the easiest because the player has to look anyway to see where the ball is before he can receive it.

8. The coach must try to build into the player each observation as it happens. Over time and with much practice the player learns to assimilate each observation more quickly until eventually they will all combine in the mind into one.

9. On reception of the ball and the ensuing success of a good first touch to control the ball the player deciding to pass the ball must think about the weight, accuracy and timing of the pass. The success or not of this can be highlighted in most of the exercises used in this book and the coach can focus on this.

10. The use of regulation soccer balls is good for these exercises but you can also use smaller soccer balls to practice.

Futsal - An Introduction

The use of the ball is based around touch, control and passing. It can't be kicked long easily and is difficult to get off the ground. The game is geared around developing fast feet and soft touches on the ball.
It is a Size Two / Three ball (regular balls are sizes 4 or 5). Due to its' smaller size, a greater degree of precision is needed to dribble and pass it but when the skills are mastered and you switch to a conventional ball these skills are easier to perform.

COACHING PRINCIPLES CONSIDERED IN THIS PROGRAM

Most of these games are not drills but are free flowing game oriented workouts aiding peripheral vision development and improving both work on and off the ball. They are Non-Directional initially and later more Directional in their make up which leads up to actual game play.

Technical

1. First touch
2. Passing - left/right, short/long
3. Control
4. Dribbling
5. Receiving and turning
6. Combination plays

Tactical

1. Positional sense (supporting)
2. Awareness
3. Communication (verbal and non-verbal)
4. Decision making (when and where)
5. Creating space
6. Understanding
7. Switching play
8. Tempo
9. Transitions

Physical

1. Speed
2. Flexibility
3. Strength (to a degree)
4. Stamina (to a degree)
5. Fitness (to a degree)

Psychological

1. Composure
2. Attitude
3. Concentration
4. Desire
5. Coachability
6. Confidence

The above principles are addressed at different levels of development depending on which particular level of progression you are working on. From a psychological sense, COMPOSURE (relaxing) and CONFIDENCE on the ball are very important to develop in a player. This helps them maintain possession instead of panicking and rushing a pass and ultimately giving possession away.

As they progress through this program you as a coach can assess when your players are ready to move to the next progression and when they are ready to cope with opposition to test their composure development. Over time you must increase their exposure to pressurizing situations so they develop this ability gradually and consistently. Do not leap from a session with no opposition where they can relax on the ball to a full-scale player for player session where the pressure is intense. Use an over-loaded practice next and gradually build up to the full-scale workout over time.

ANTICIPATION / IMAGINATION / AWARENESS
KEY POINTS CHECKLIST AND BASIC SET UP

1. **Head Up** (avoid looking down at the ball and consequently not observing what is around and where players are in relation to each other).

2. **Looking Before Receiving** - anticipating the next pass before you receive the ball thinking ahead, looking over your shoulder,(eyes in the back of your head!!). Equate it with the younger players to a bird on a fence looking around. This gives the player a better chance of retaining possession and not getting caught on the ball by an opponent.

3. **Body Stance Open**, side on, half turned for greater peripheral vision plus moving off at an angle to receive, not supporting in a straight line (the angle and distance of support is crucial so you can see most if not all players to pass to).

4. **First Touch** - Move the ball on your first touch away from pressure (good first touch is crucial). Relaxation in your body as you receive the ball is imperative. For younger players you can liken the cushion of the body part to catching an egg.

5. **Verbal Communication** - Use words during the practices (and in games) to help the receiver.
   a) Can be "**Man On**" - to simulate a situation in a non-competitive practice so the player doesn't turn, but plays the way they are facing.
   b) "**Turn**", helps the player to turn and thus switch the point of attack by letting the ball run across the body. The passer must see there is space behind the receiver for them to move in.
   c) "**Time**" so the players on the ball know they can take 2 or 3 touches if they need to.

6. **Changing Pace** - Changing pace on reception of the ball because the player may need to get away from a defender (quick burst into space with the ball).

7. **Changing Direction** - Turning or moving off at angles on reception of the ball. This provides a basis to work from but using your imagination you can develop other ideas that can be applied in this session and be equally effective.

8. **Support** - Once you have made a pass, look to support others in possession to receive again (avoids standing admiring your pass and hence be out of the game). Then we deal with angle and distance of support again. Look to move to support the next pass as the ball is traveling to a teammate. Move to the ball if receiving it to feet to save time and prevent opponents from intercepting the pass.

9. **No Communication** - a test for players to make them think for themselves with no verbal or non-verbal help (no calls of man on, turn or pointing). This helps their own awareness greatly.

10. **Switching Play** - by letting the ball run across your body to change direction and switch play, saving a touch using upper body to disguise your movement (leaning one way to throw a feint and moving in the opposite direction). Use the pace of the pass to help you and recognize the space to move into before you receive the pass.

11. **Determine Length of Pass** - short or long tries to include variation. Deal with the weight, accuracy and timing of the pass.

12. **Determine Type of Work** on the ball e.g. turns, dribbles, 1 - 2's, passes, one touch, two touch, crossovers, all after receiving etc.

13. **Big First Touch** - out of your feet into space away from the pressure on receiving. Player must recognize this space before he / she receives the ball.

14. **Fitness** - Pass the ball then run to the furthest line of the area you are working in (sprint work). This also helps spread players out.

15. **One Touch - Two-Touch play**, particularly One touch, looking for the support player to work an angle off the receiving player so the ball can be laid off one touch. In this we are working on the support player's position as well as the player on the ball (thinking two moves ahead).

16. **Passing to Feet** - The receiver must move to the ball along the line of the pass, **not stand still** (in a game, standing still almost invites an opponent to intercept the pass). Moving to the ball to receive can help prevent this from happening.

ANTICIPATION, IMAGINATION, AWARENESS

17. **Passing to Space**, forcing the movement of the receiver by a pass to space. It can be the passer dictating where he wants the receiver to go or the receiver pointing to show the passer where he wants the ball to go. Both need to recognize where the space is to play the ball to. When passing to space, the passer must weight the pass correctly, be accurate with it and have correct timing.

18. **Crossovers** - principles are: using inside foot to exchange, take / leave ball, use as a decoy, accelerate away, communication.

19. **Playing Give and Go's** - two teams, one team with a ball each, the other without balls, passing and playing 1- 2's. Emphasize one or two touch lay off and passing into space so the player doesn't need to break stride as he receives the return pass. To begin, have players without the ball standing still, then as they improve have them moving to play 1-2's.

20. **Passing** - Concentrate on the weight, accuracy and timing of the passes depending on: the distances the ball is being played, whether it is to feet or space, the positioning of the other teams players (simulating defensive organization), the positioning of your own team-mates.

GAME PROGRESSIONS

1. Basic Set Up - Two Teams, one ball, passing to anyone. Then two balls passing to anyone.

2. Two teams / two balls, one per team passing only to own teammates, passing through the other team (half the number of passing choices compared to the last progression).
Develop as follows:

a) Number of touches on the ball; fewer means the ball must be moved more quickly. Go all in to start, then three, two and eventually one touch passing (but have the restriction as a guide). As number of touches decreases, the ability needed to anticipate the next pass and where it should go increases. Insist that they only play one touch if it is on to do so as it isn't always the correct choice to make.

b) Size of area: tighter means closer control needed.

c) Number of balls per team up to 50 / 50 ratio.1 ball to two players per team e.g. 12 players, 6 balls. Work on 1 - 2's, crossovers etc.

d) Make it Competitive; have a time period over which each team must maintain possession of the ball or balls. If a ball runs out of the area (thus possession is lost) or bumps into another ball then the other team gets a point. Start with the teams in different areas then as they improve have them play in the same area to increase the difficulty. Increase the difficulty by going two touch (if a player uses more than two touches the other team get a point). Use your imagination to invent new scenarios for this.

3. Two teams / two balls, passing to opposite colors (other team). Color discrimination, passing in sequence, vision. Increase to four balls; two per team. Four teams of 3 players / one ball each group.
Develop as follows :

a) Go to free spaces to receive and pass the ball to another teammate of the same color. Three or two touch play. If the ball is passed to another color, this player must pass it back one / two touch to the same player he received it from.
b) Coach signals, players sprint in four directions to corners of the grid and continue passing to each other. Do the same but different colors in each corner (three in each). Quick reflexes, color vision required.

ANTICIPATION, IMAGINATION, AWARENESS

These exercises allow a flow rate to happen regarding **PASSING** and **SUPPORT** and help players to develop **CONFIDENCE** and **COMPOSURE** on the ball. Development can be monitored and progression can be clearly judged. The coach can move the players onto the next level when they recognize the time is right. I have carefully developed the levels of progression of these sessions to ensure each level is addressed at the correct time.

BASIC SESSION IN THREES

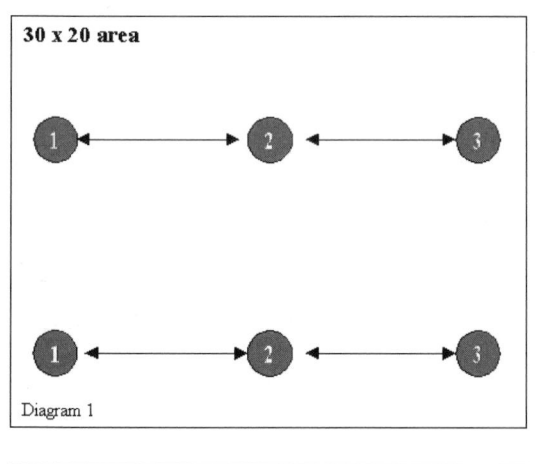

Diagram 1

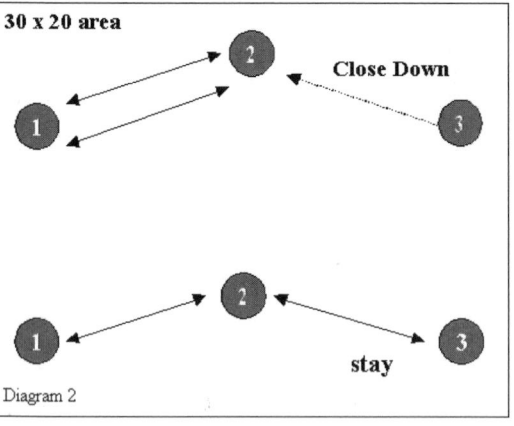

Diagram 2

1 passes to 2
2 passes to 3

Coaching Points

1. Look over shoulder before receiving (where you are passing)

2. Body Stance - half turned (can see behind)

3. Support at an angle.

4. Save a touch - let weight of ball determine this - let it run across body and move one touch

5. Develop - Opposite player stays or closes the middle player down

6. If closed down, middle player passes back to the player who passed to him

7. If not closed down, the middle player turns and passes to opposite player

PROGRESSIVE AWARENESS SESSION IN THREES

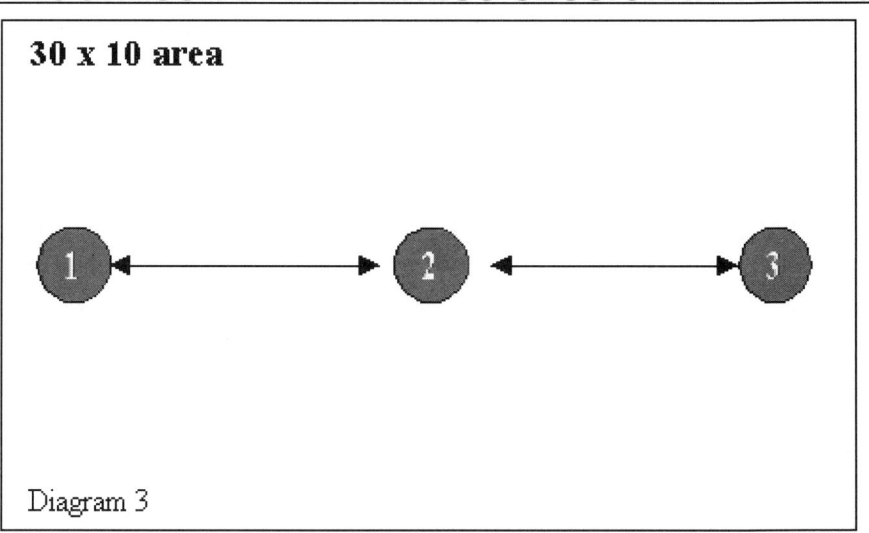

30 x 10 area

Diagram 3

Go through each progression in the order it is presented here. Do one at a time and have each player practice in the middle at every stage of the progressions.

1. Begin by passing the ball from (1) to (2) to (3) and back. (2) Receives and turns and passes. Passing must be sharp and accurate, one or two touch. (Diagram 3)

2. You can receive with the foot **furthest** away from the passer and pass it with the nearest foot, or save a touch and move it one touch with the inside of the nearest foot or the outside of the furthest foot. Let the weight of the pass determine this, let it run across your body and move it **one** touch.

3. The player in the middle must **open** his body stance by going side on so he can see what is behind him. This makes it easier to receive and pass the ball on.

4. Look over the shoulder to see what's behind, do this **before** receiving the ball, not after.

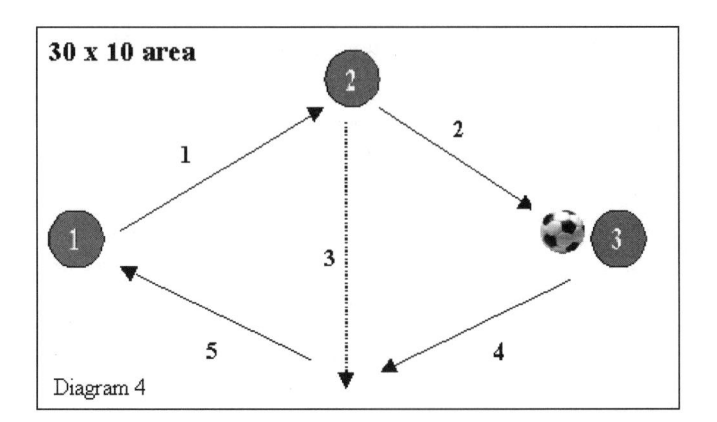

Diagram 4

5. Position in the middle **off at an angle** to receive, this makes a triangular support position and opens up the field of vision. Once the ball has been passed on, the middle player moves to the other side off at an angle again (can use cones to run to both sides). This forces the players to receive and pass with both feet. (Diagram 4)

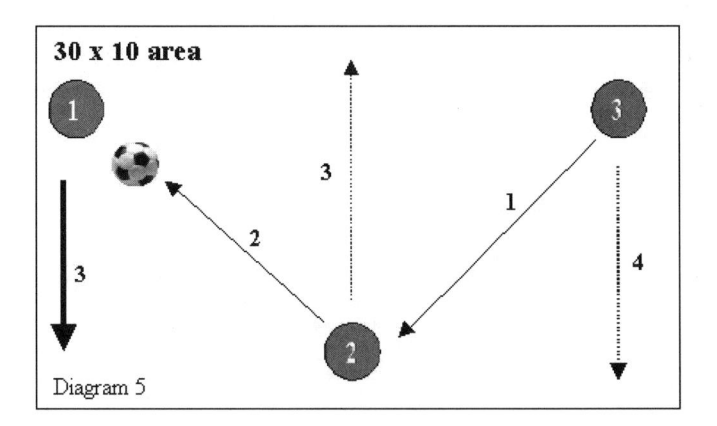

Diagram 5

6. Now working on the movement of the outside player to create a bigger angle to pass and receive the ball. Above (2) passes to (1) who moves the ball into space with a good first touch to pass the ball back with a second touch. (Diagram 5) The movement is shown on the following page. Likewise (3) receives and moves the ball off at an angle and the cycle continues. (Diagram 6)

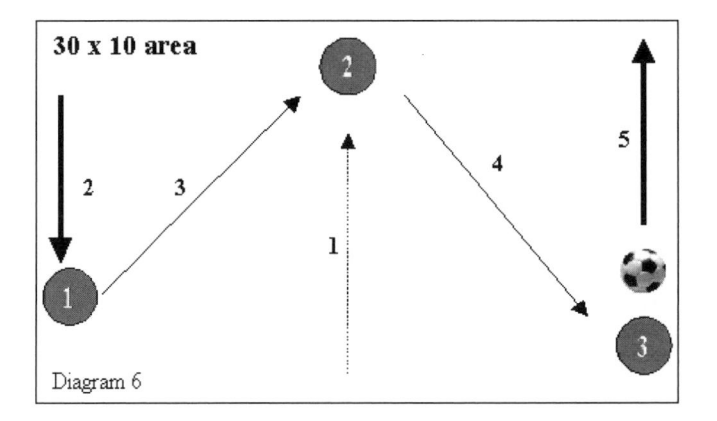

Diagram 6

7. Working on the middle player again : if he is marked, he should look to come short to receive the pass to get away from the defender. (Diagram 7)

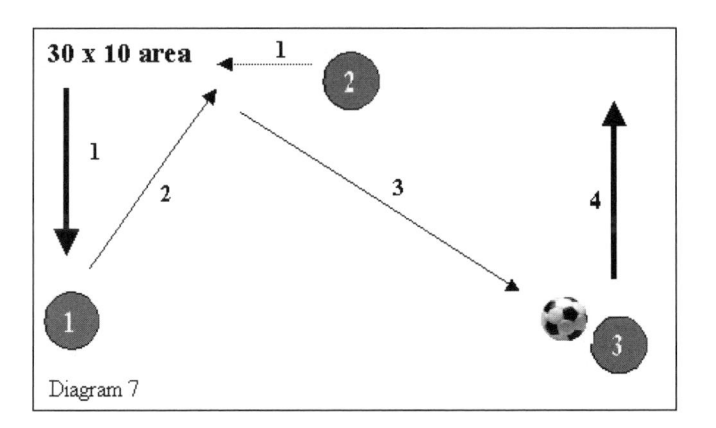

Diagram 7

8. Moving short to receive the pass; in a game it is getting away from the defender to receive in space with time on the ball. Keep the angle wide so you can still receive the pass side on. If you move short but more central you will receive the ball more with your back to the play with less room to work the ball in. (Diagram 8)

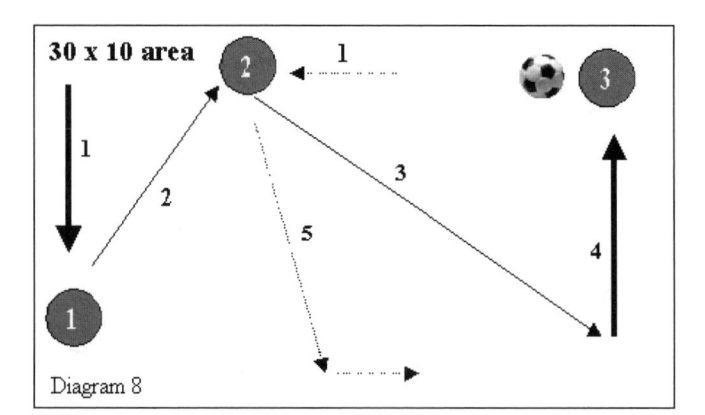

Diagram 8

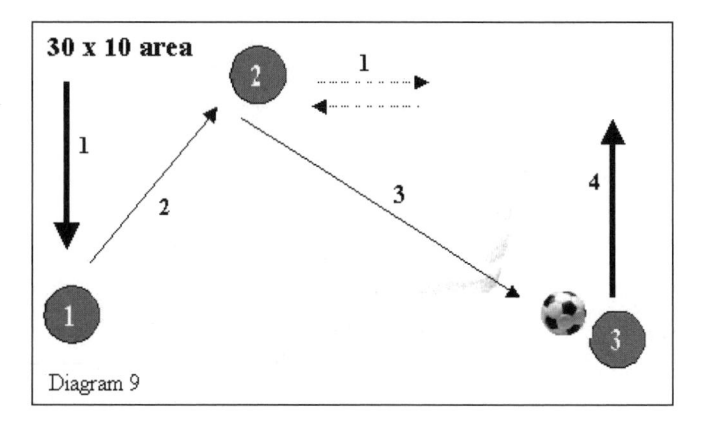

Diagram 9

9. Develop by the middle player moving away from the ball to take a defender away from the space and then checking back to receive the pass in time and space. (Diagram 9)

10. With these movements the passer must be aware of the receiver's movements to get the timing of the pass right. The receiver must be aware of how quickly the passer has control of the ball and be ready to pass it to get the timing of the run correct (therefore always looking).

11. These movements in a game are dictated by how much time on the ball the passer has, if no time then coming short to receive the first pass, if time on the ball then the receiver can run a defender off the check and receive to feet.

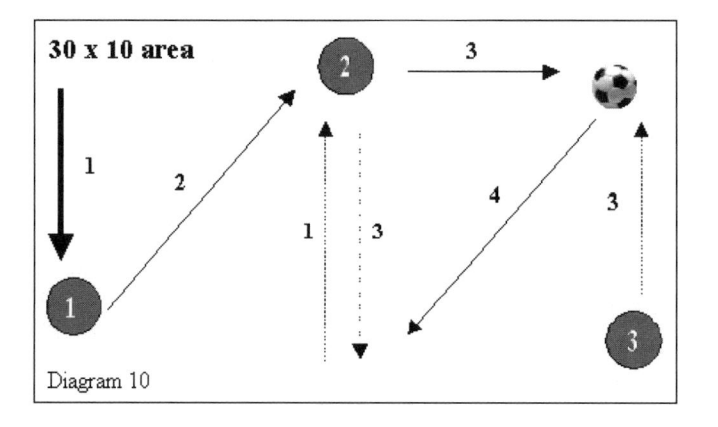

Diagram 10

12. The middle player receives the ball and passes into space to move the outside player. Previously it was a pass to feet and the outside player moved the ball. (Diagram 10)

13. The opposite outside player from the ball can decide to close down the middle player or stay away. If he closes down then the middle player must pass the ball back to the player who passed it to him. If he stays in position then the middle player passes the ball to him. This shows whether the player has checked the other players' positions before receiving the pass. Put a passive defender in with the middle player to show how to check off and lose the marker. (Diagrams 11 and 12)

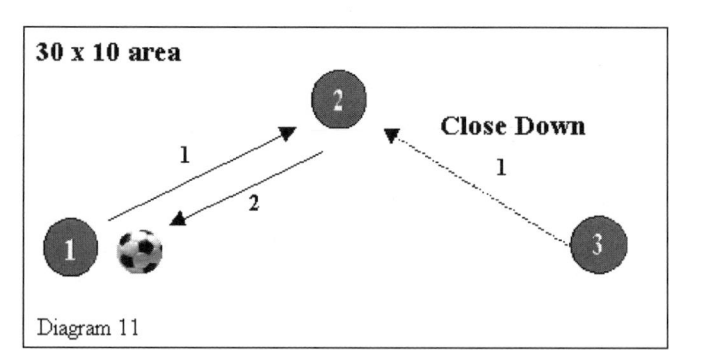

Diagram 11

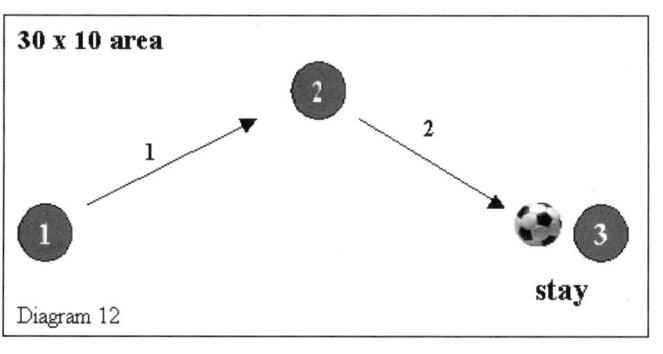

Diagram 12

ANTICIPATION, IMAGINATION, AWARENESS

RECEIVING, CONTROLLING AND TURNING WITH THE BALL

1. Support in a diagonal position, not in a straight line (off at an angle).

2. Receivers face the player with the ball (eye contact) so they know the receiver is ready.

3. Receiver moves **to** the ball to avoid anticipation of a defender intercepting or **away** to create space to come back into.

4. Receiver is aware of where the space is to turn. Body position half turned to receive while moving the ball on the first touch (changing direction). Use upper body to create an element of surprise or disguise.

5. Get your body between the ball and your opponent (screen the ball).

6. On receiving and changing direction with the first touch, change pace (away from a defender).

7. Use your arms to protect yourself and keep your knees bent for good balance.

IN FOURS

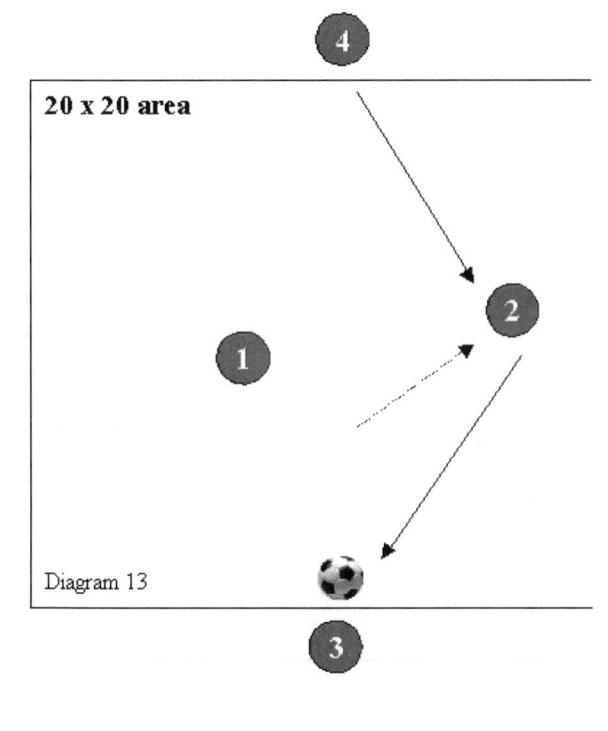

20 x 20 area

Diagram 13

1. No opposition to begin.

2. (4) Passes to (2) who receives, controls and passes to (3). (1) Receives from (3), turns and passes to (4) and so on. Rotate the players in the middle.

3. Have the other player in the middle be a passive defender.

4. Middle players can switch sides to receive and turn.

5. Turning inside and turning outside using inside and outside of the foot (practicing with both feet).

ANTICIPATION, IMAGINATION, AWARENESS

IN FOURS

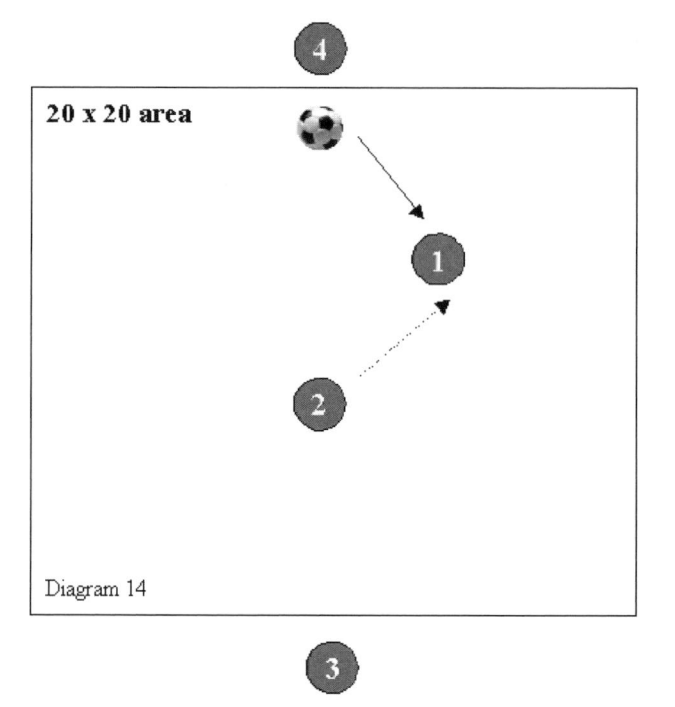

Diagram 14

1. Introduce a defender. (1) Must receive and turn and pass to (3), (2) tries to stop the play. Can pass back and move again. Work both directions.

2. Methods of Turning :

a) Check off, receive and turn inside and face up to defender in one movement off first touch.
b) Receiver backs into defender and receives ball to feet, spinning defender using his body as a screen.
c) Turn away with outside / inside of each foot.
d) Turning without the ball, pull defender short creating space behind, spin quickly and take the ball behind the defender or play 1-2 and go.
e) Run defender off away from the ball then check back into space you have created to receive.

IN EIGHTS

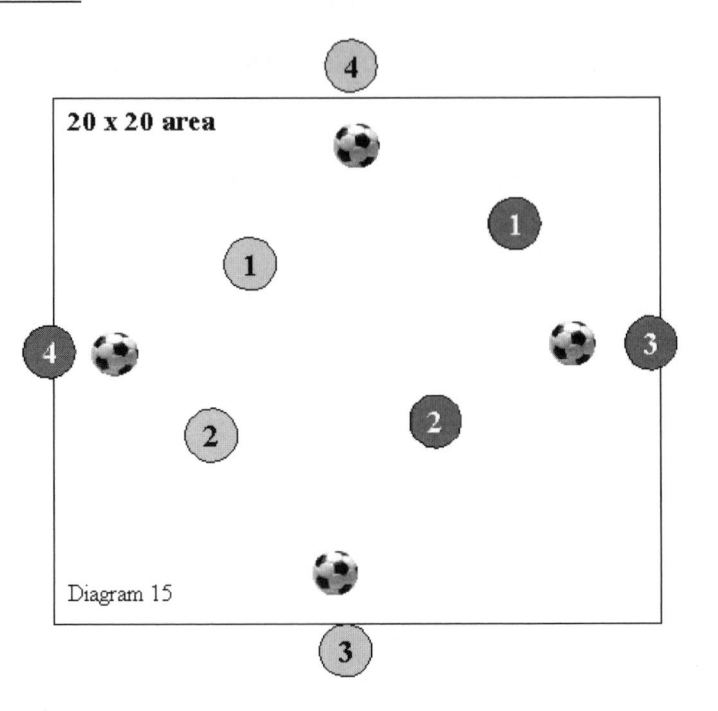

Diagram 15

1. Inside player receives from one outside player and passes to another free outside player.

2. Outside player moves the ball side to side to keep working until a pass is on. Rotate. Use different turns using all coaching points. Determine touches on the ball for quickness of turn.

IMPROVING SPATIAL AWARENESS: AN INTRODUCTION

To begin, build up the session slowly, one team only without a ball.

1. Players move around the zone finding space. Coach calls "stop", players stop, check positions. They shouldn't be too near each other, showing they recognize how to use the spaces in the zone.

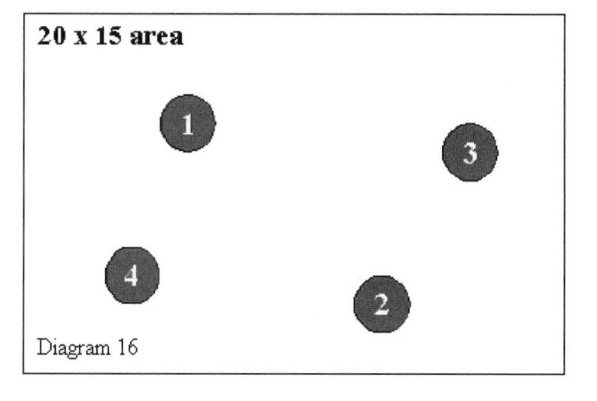

20 x 15 area

Diagram 16

2. Ask players to move again and call a shape they need to form, e.g. a diamond, a square, a straight line. This indicates how quickly they can form a team shape. Look to maintain equal distances between each other.

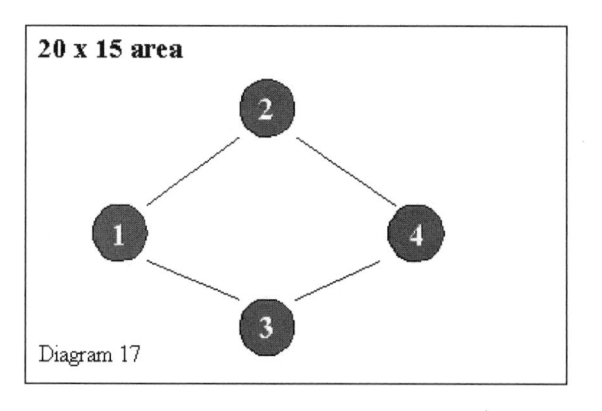

20 x 15 area

Diagram 17

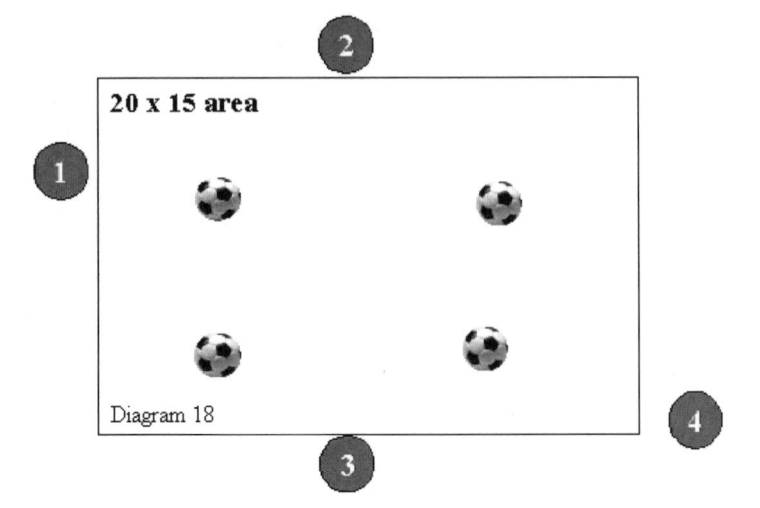

Diagram 18

3. Add a ball each and do the above two exercises but on calling "stop", (or getting them into a shape and stopping) ask the players to run out of the area and check where the balls are in terms of spatial awareness or team shape (e.g. a square).

4. Add another team and continue the process.

   a) You can practice passing with hands to work support positions.
   b) Two teams, one with a ball for each player, one team without a ball. On a call, have the team with a ball each pass to the other team and then continue the movement.
   c) Two teams, a ball each team passing and moving.

GROUP RHYTHM AND MOVEMENT (IN FIVES)

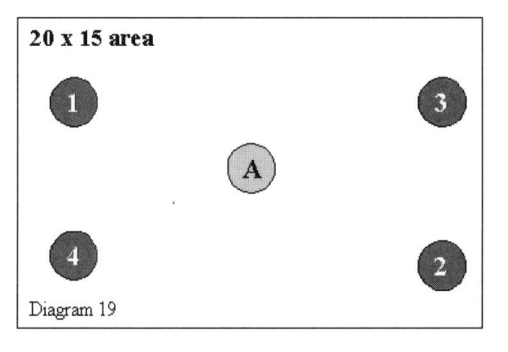

Diagram 19

1. Lay four cones down for reference.

2. Exchange corners, player in the middle must beat someone to a corner.

3. Introduce a ball for each player.

GROUP RHYTHM AND MOVEMENT ON A LARGER SCALE (4-4-2)

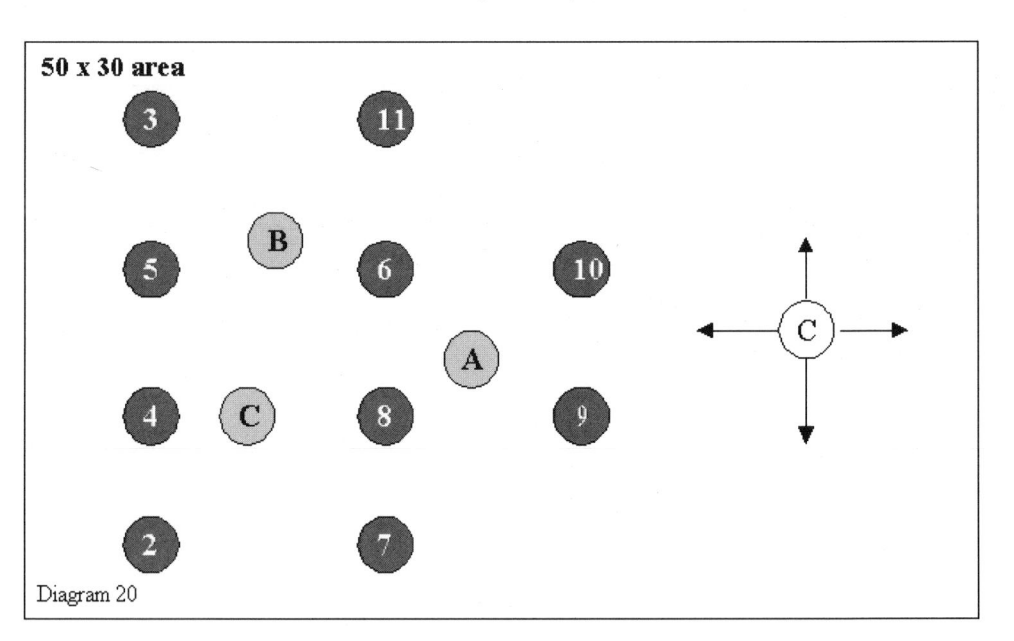

Diagram 20

1. Players' movements mirror the coach. Four directions: left and right, forward and back, running on the spot otherwise.

2. Introduce three players who try to get to a cone as the players move between them. Learning the concepts of **SPACE**, **TIME**, and **ORIENTATION** in the **RHYTHM** and **MOVEMENT** of the players.

ANTICIPATION, IMAGINATION, AWARENESS

GROUP RHYTHM WITH TEAMS CHANGING FORMATIONS

Teams change around quickly on the call of the coach to adjust to the new team shape.

3-4-1-2

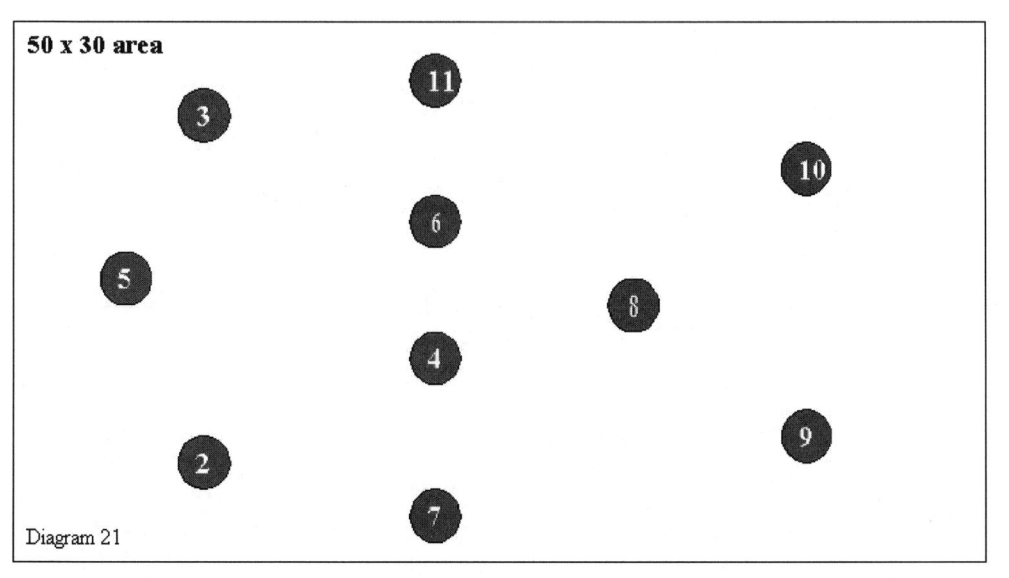

4-3-1-2

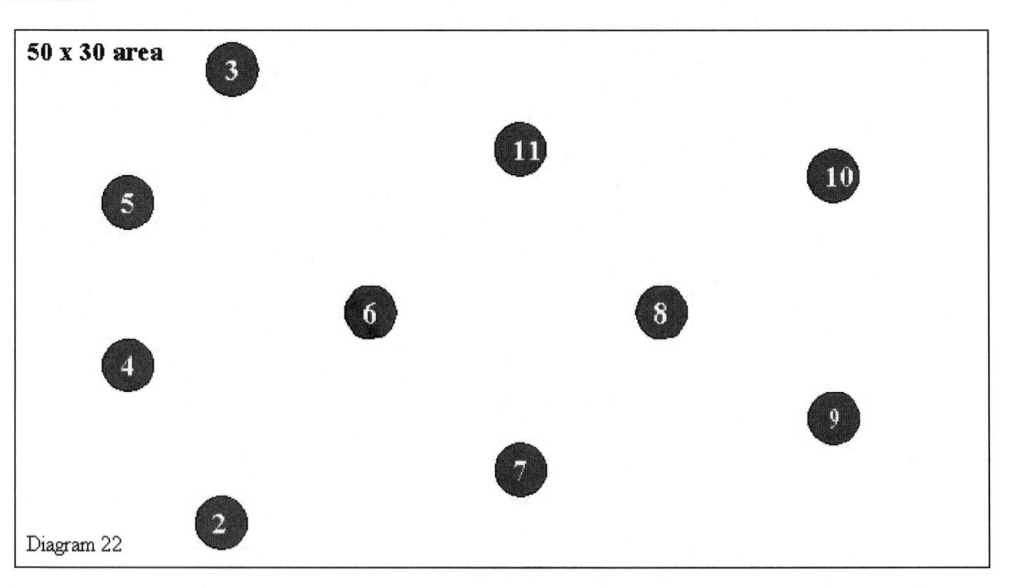

3-1-4-2

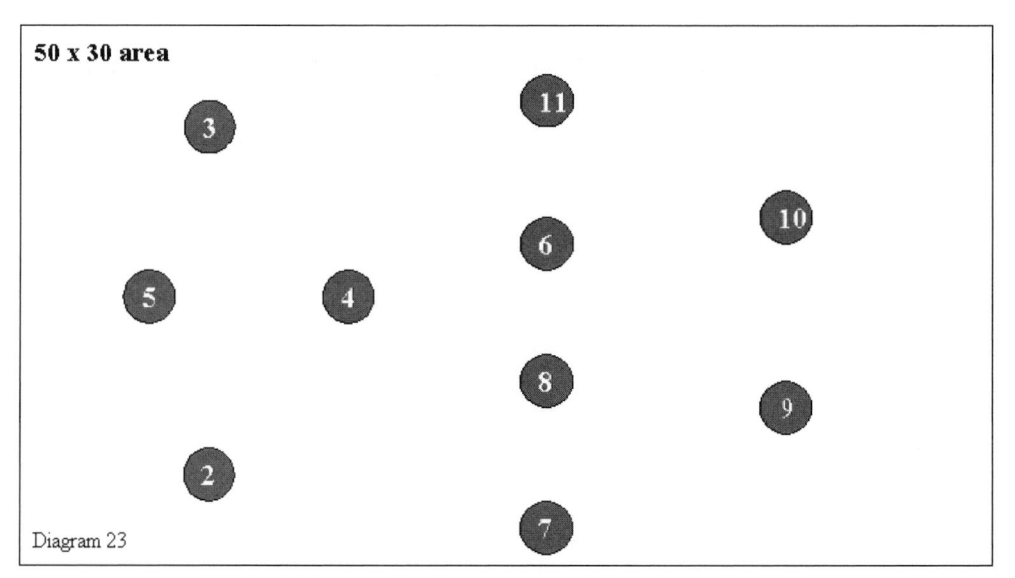

4-3-1-2 (The Christmas Tree Formation)

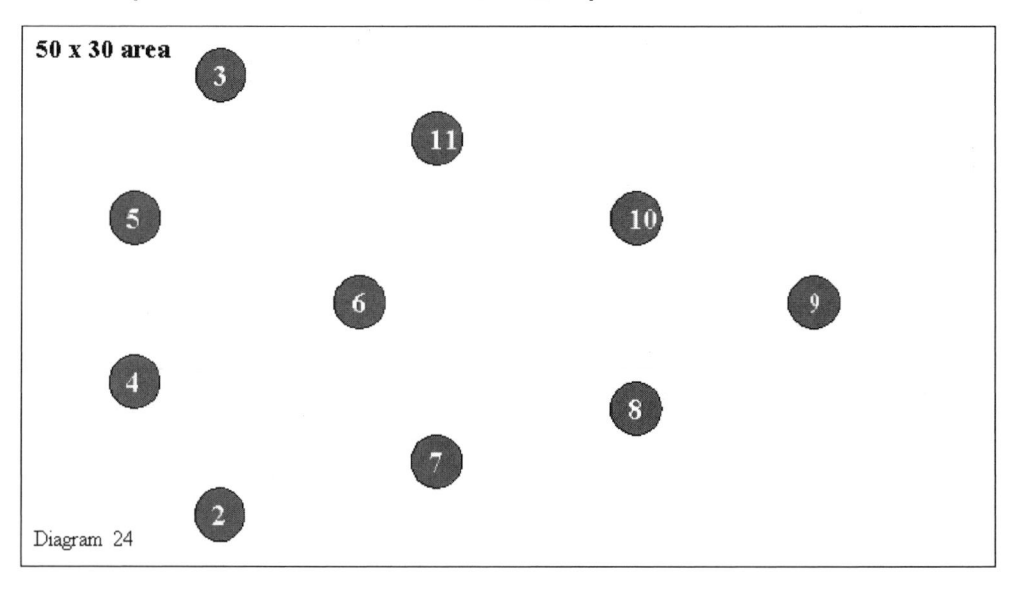

AWARENESS WITH A BALL EACH

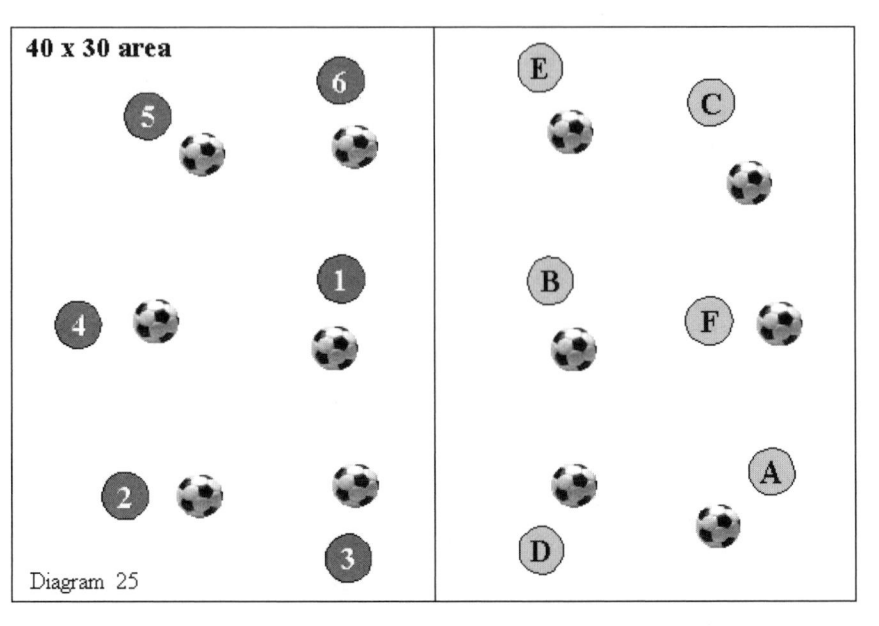

Diagram 25

1. Moving around with the ball, staying in **space**. Stop and check positions. Check how **spread out** players are. Discuss the implications of being in possession of the ball in a game and making it hard for the opposition to mark you by using as much width and length as possible. The players learn to use the spaces as effectively as possible.

2. Continue with dribbling but emphasize keeping the **head up** and **not looking at the ball** but looking around, in front, side to side and behind (for younger players equate it to a bird on a fence looking around). The players can see the ball in their **peripheral vision** without looking at it directly.

3. Emphasize **awareness** of where other players are who are working in the same area by looking around; in front, to the side, and behind.

4. You can include switching play by the coach calling "**switch**" where balls are stopped and players must take someone else's ball and continue dribbling. This determines who has quick awareness of where the free balls are.

IDENTIFYING LEVELS OF AWARENESS

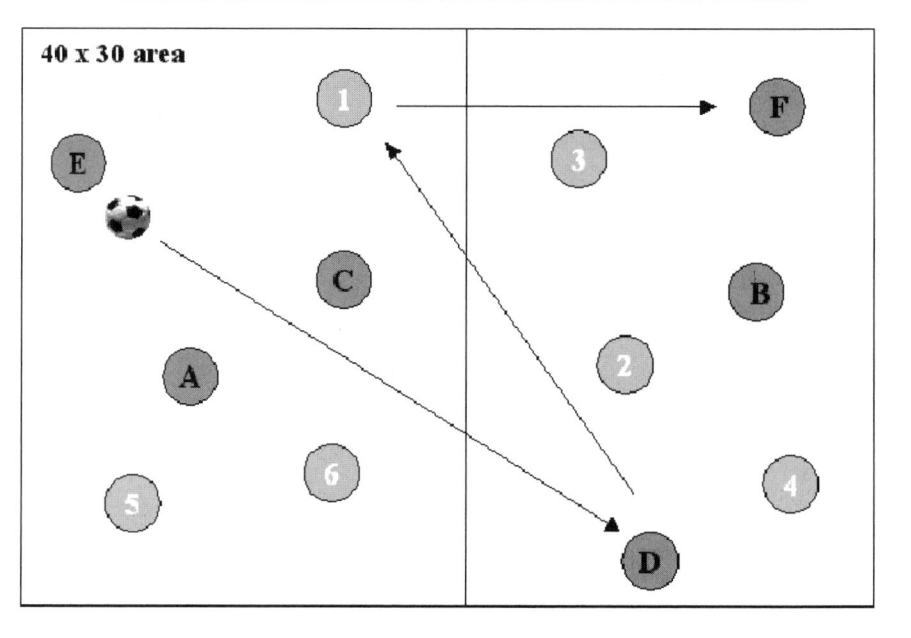

1. Have the players stand still and pass the ball around the group. They must **look** before they receive the ball to see where they are passing. Make it 2 then 1 touch.

2. To ensure they are looking, have them call the name of the player they are passing to before they pass the ball. When they don't call the name you know they haven't looked ahead of the ball.

3. Observe which players can't do this and allow them 2 touches and more time and look to see how they improve with practice.

4. **Develop** - Two teams pass to opposite colors so the choices are halved. The players have to be even more aware of where they are passing to before they receive the ball.

5. Introduce 2 balls to the session then 3 and so on, but players continue to stand still to keep it simple to get success.

6. Have them begin to move around the area slowly to make the decision making more difficult.

FOUR TEAM PASSING GAME INTRODUCTION

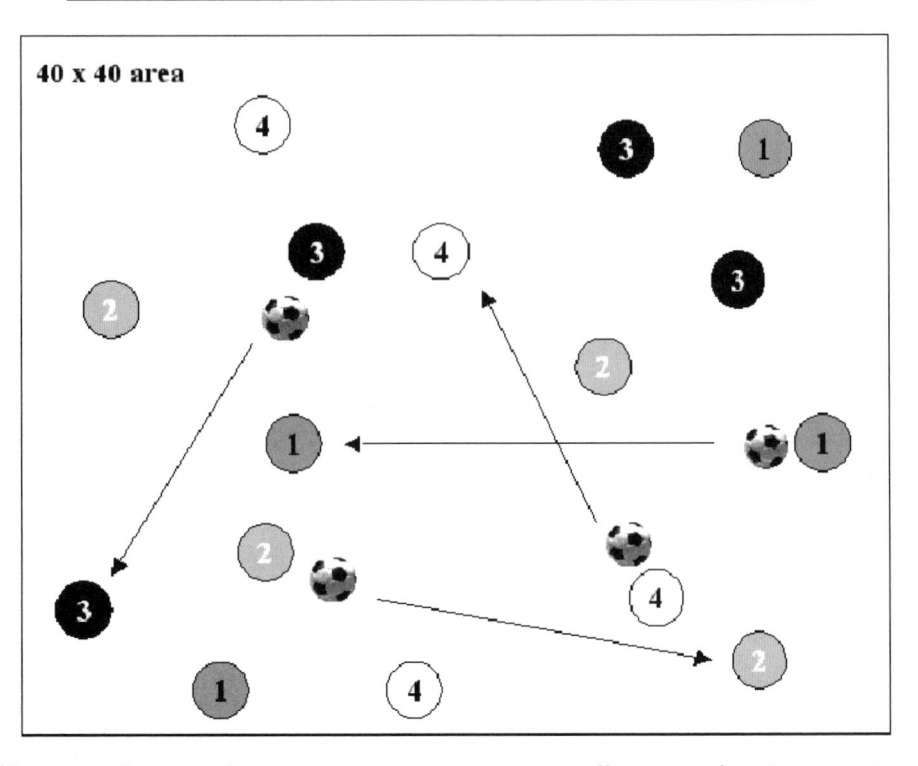

40 x 40 area

1. Sixteen players, four teams, everyone standing passing to own team, moving a yard or so to each side to make an angle to receive the pass if a player from the other team gets in the path of the ball.

2. Generally, players should stand still so it's easy to find a teammate, making an easy introduction to the session.

3. Move the ball on the first touch, opening up the angle to make the next pass.

4. Players have to call the name of the player they are passing to before they release the ball to show they have seen that player early in a support position.

5. Make it one touch so they really have to look before receiving. When this becomes easy and players get success they then are allowed to move around the area so it is more difficult to find a teammate. Restrict number of touches to increase difficulty again.

6. You can see from this session who has grasped the concept of looking before receiving and who needs more work.

ANTICIPATION, IMAGINATION, AWARENESS

COMPETITIVE FOUR TEAM GAME

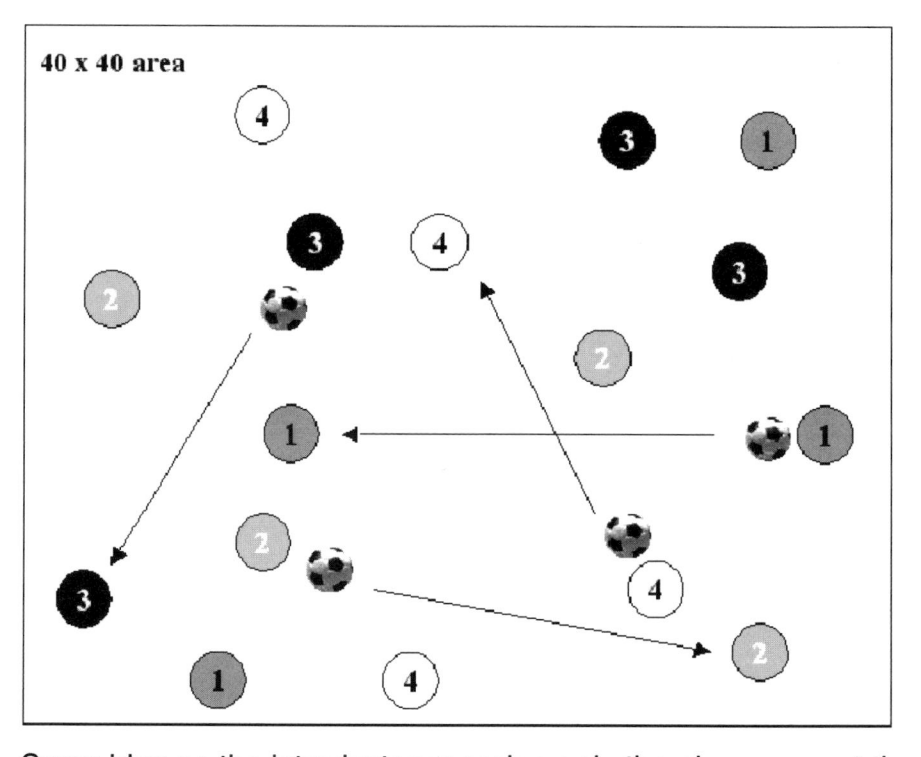

1. Same idea as the introductory session only the players count the number of passes they make in a given time. Compare the totals. They can't pass back to the same player they received from.

2. Introduce several small goals for the players to pass through and count the number of goals scored. Ensure the players arrive at the goal (timing of the run) as the ball is passed through the goal (timing of the pass).

3. Players must not stand by a goal waiting for a pass as in a game they as they would be easily marked.

4. **Develop** - Increase the number of goals per team (two balls per team). Combine two teams and have them passing to the other color and have three balls going at once. The variations can be numerous.

ANTICIPATION, IMAGINATION, AWARENESS

KEEPING BALANCE IN ZONES ENSURING MOVEMENT OFF THE BALL

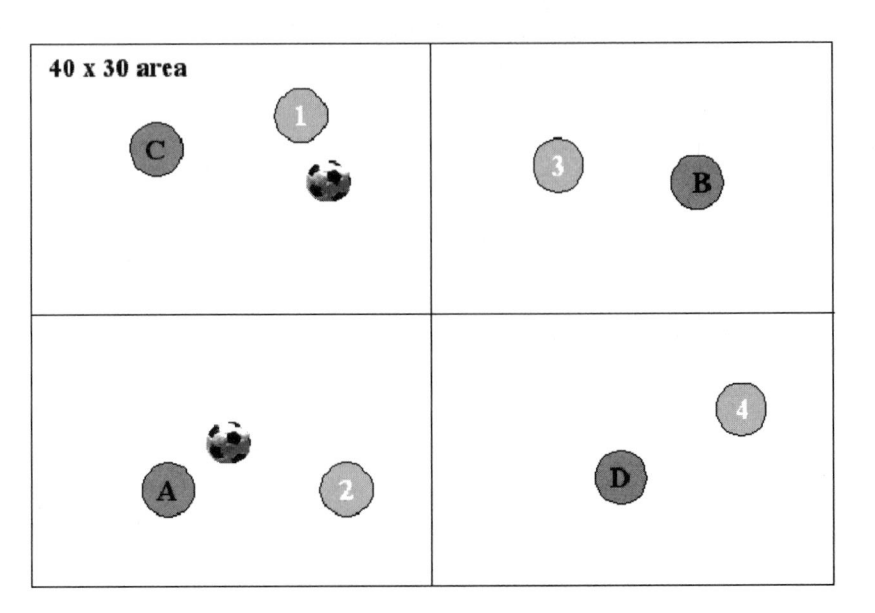

A player must be in each zone so as one moves in, one moves out ensuring movement on and off the ball. Above session is a four zone game. Below is a six zone game with more potential movement from the players.

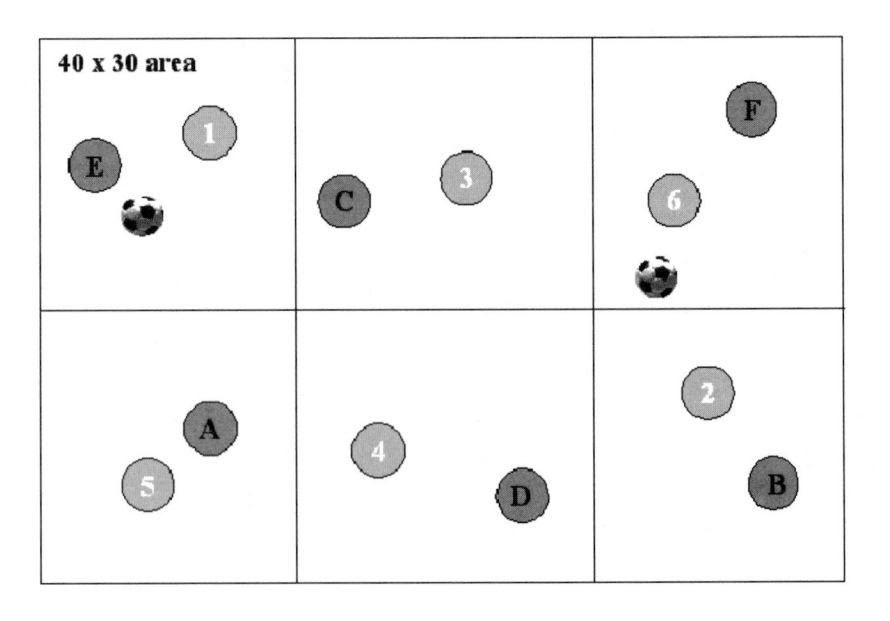

SIMPLE INTRODUCTION TO THE ANTICIPATION, IMAGINATION AND AWARENESS SESSION

This practice is designed to allow the players to be gently introduced to the fundamentals of the A.I.A. session, enabling them to practice without too much movement.

TWO TEAM SET-UP

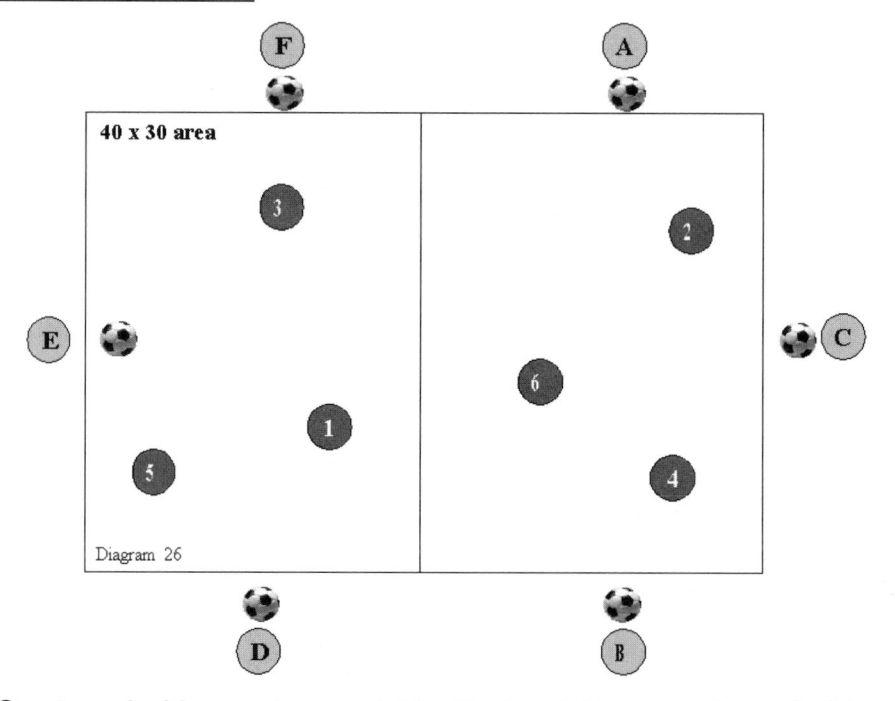

Diagram 26

1. One team inside, one team outside. Each outside player has a ball to begin.

2. Outside players pass to an inside player who receives and turns and finds another outside free player with a pass, then looks to receive from another outside player.

3. The outside player receives and moves the ball side to side until another inside player is free to receive a pass. This ensures all the players are working both inside and outside the grid.

4. Change the practice to all inside players with a ball. These players now look to pass and receive a give and go from an outside player.

5. Rotate the players so both teams have the chance to play in the middle of the grid.

6. Move both teams to the middle, divide the grid into two with each team passing to their own team within their own grid area, keeping teams separate to begin.

ANTICIPATION, IMAGINATION, AWARENESS

ANTICIPATION/IMAGINATION/AWARENESS SESSION

1. This is the **basic beginning** of the A.I.A. session (following on from the introductory practice) where we first have all the players moving **freely**, passing and moving within their own team. Divide the group into two teams again. Begin with one ball being passed around a team and as they become proficient introduce another ball to increase their A.I.A. qualities. A ratio of approximately one ball per three players is ideal.

2. Introduce the other team that has been practicing in another grid and have the two teams play **through** each other but **not against** each other.

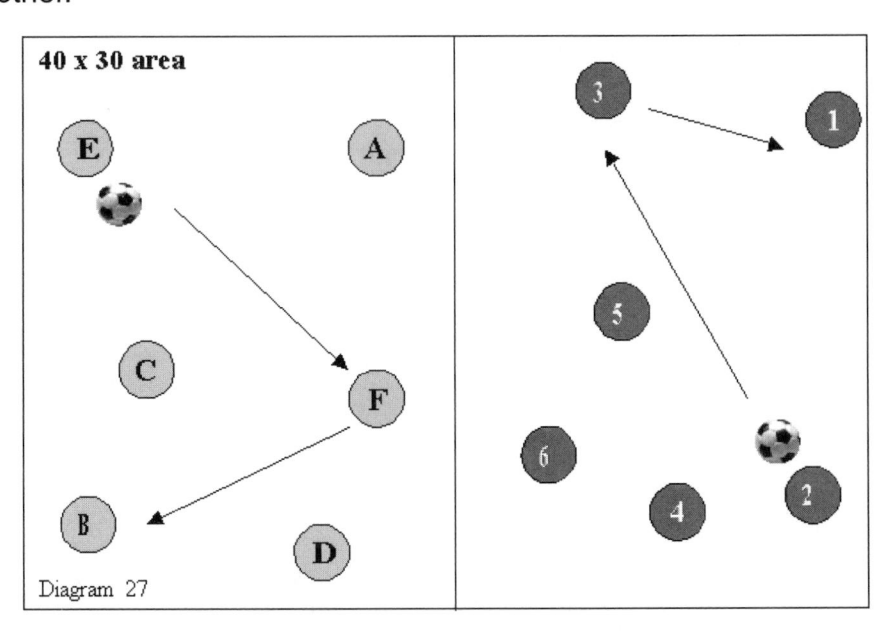

Diagram 27

3. Have the teams play throughout both grids to spread the play out and get the players comfortable and composed. As they improve you can change it to playing in one grid only so there is less room to work in and things happen more quickly. This is a test of their A.I.A. ability.

4. The Technical / Tactical Design within the framework of the session is described on page 34.

5. As the players gain proficiency, you can introduce new situations for them to deal with, all of which will be covered later. You may need to spend time repeating this basic set up before you move on the other situational work. Be patient and ensure they get the basics right first.

6. Develop - Have 4 teams playing through each other, players passing to their own teammates.

Combine 2 teams with different colors and have them passing to the other color.

7. Ultimately, for example, red passes to blue, blue to green, green to yellow, yellow to red. This increases their awareness of where teammates are positioned to pass to.

TWO TEAMS PLAYING THROUGH EACH OTHER

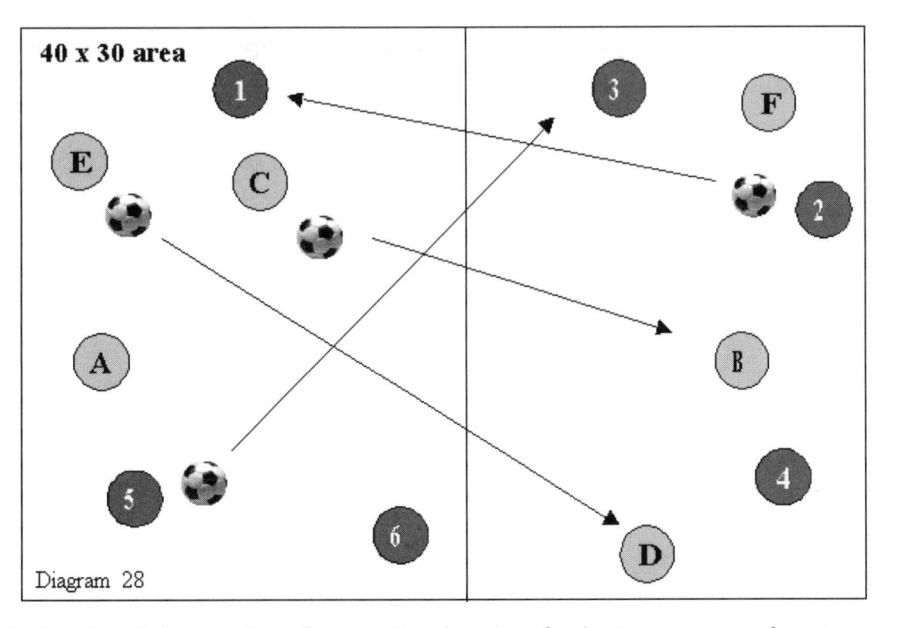

Diagram 28

The following information forms the basis of what we are trying to achieve with this session. More information will be added later to progress the work we are doing here.

Technical / Tactical Design

a) The players must play with their heads up (so they view what is around).

b) Look over the shoulder before receiving the ball.

c) Body stance open to receive the ball.

d) Awareness of teammates' positions on the field.

e) Awareness of opponents' positions on the field.

f) Move the ball on the first touch away from pressure into space (or 1 touch transfer).

g) Passing to space to move players into a better position on the field.

h) Passing to the player's feet.

i) Turns / dribbles / 1t / 2t / free play etc.

j) Communication (verbal, physical or through eye contact).

k) Angles / distances of support.

l) Passer pressures receiver by closing him down after the pass.

m) Receiver moves the ball away at an angle off the first touch.

ANTICIPATION, IMAGINATION, AWARENESS

As you practice with your team, don't try to develop all the key coaching points in one session. It may be you have to spend several sessions on just establishing the first key point of getting the players to play with their head up and not looking down at the ball.

Once you believe you are getting success with this, only then must you move to working on the second point in your next practices.

This process of learning is the same as in the introduction where there are several things the player must think about even before they receive the ball beginning with seeing where the ball is coming from and so on up to the selection of the pass.

PASSING TO OPPOSITE COLORS

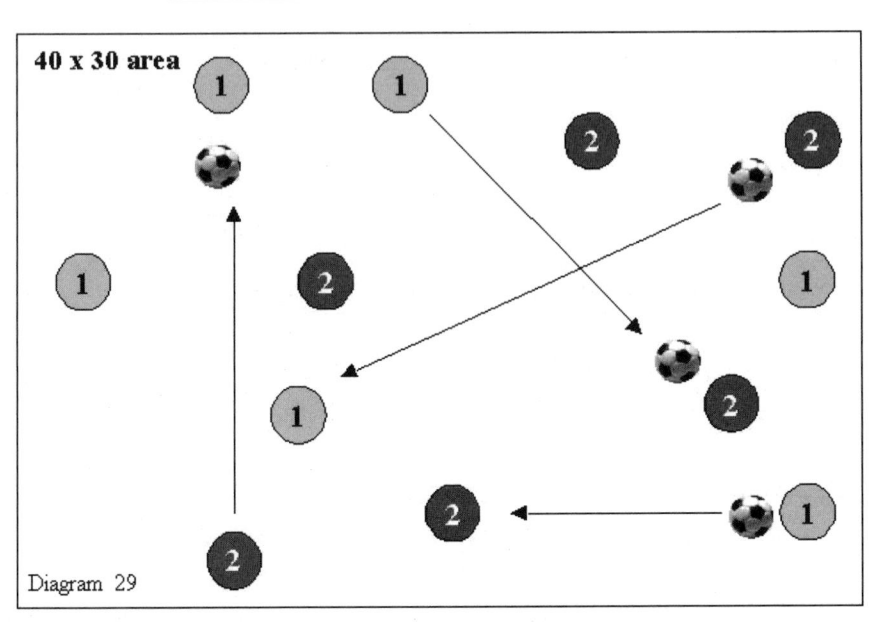

Diagram 29

FOUR TEAMS WITH A BALL EACH TEAM

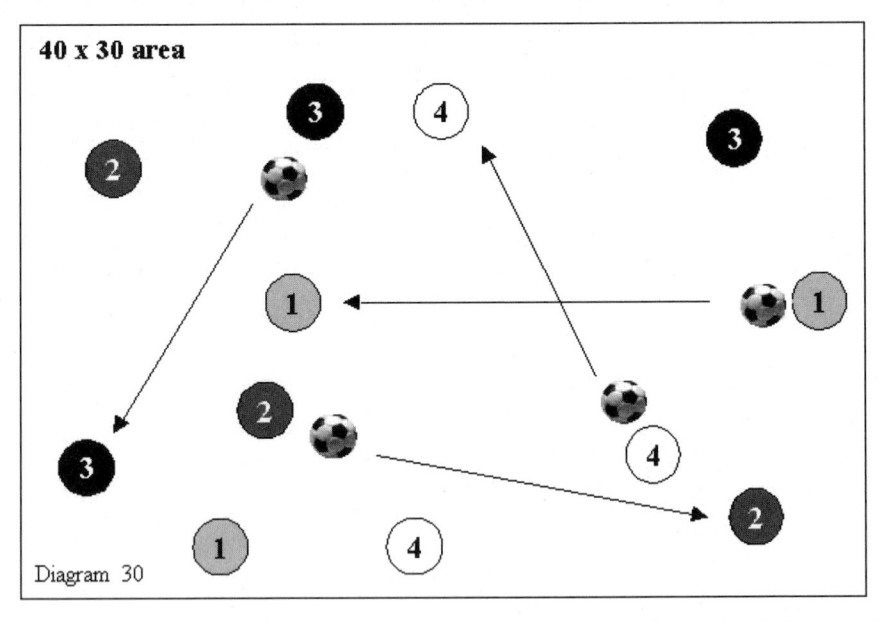

Diagram 30

1. To further test the players' ability to look beyond the ball, have the players take off their pinnies. The players know who is in their team, but must really look to distinguish them from the other players.

2. Getting good at this means they play in their team with their team-mates in the same color. It is easier to pick out teammates and keep possession of the ball.

ANTICIPATION, IMAGINATION, AWARENESS

COACH SIGNALS: PLAYERS SPLIT UP IN TEAMS

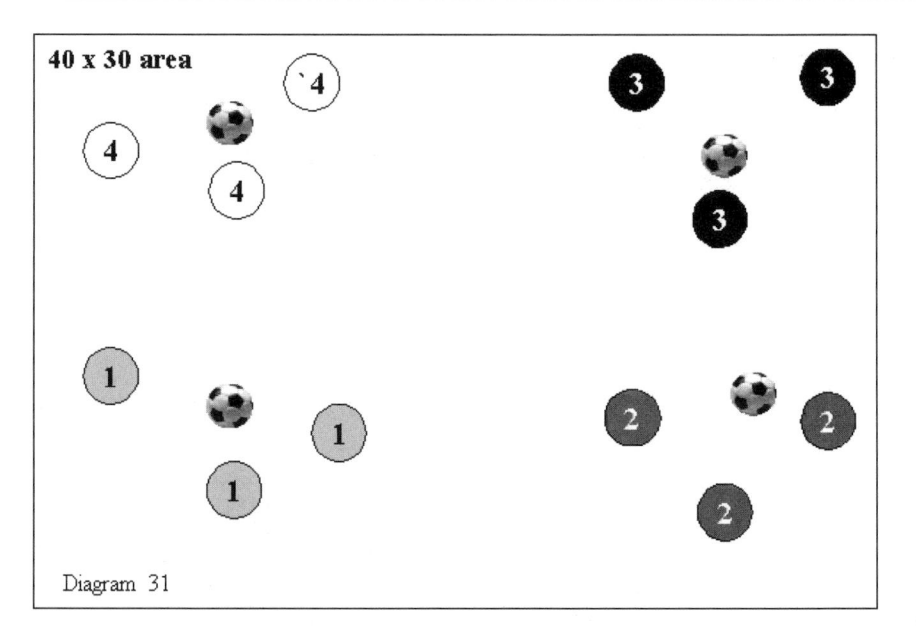

Diagram 31

COACH SIGNALS: PLAYERS IN TEAMS OF DIFFERENT COLORS

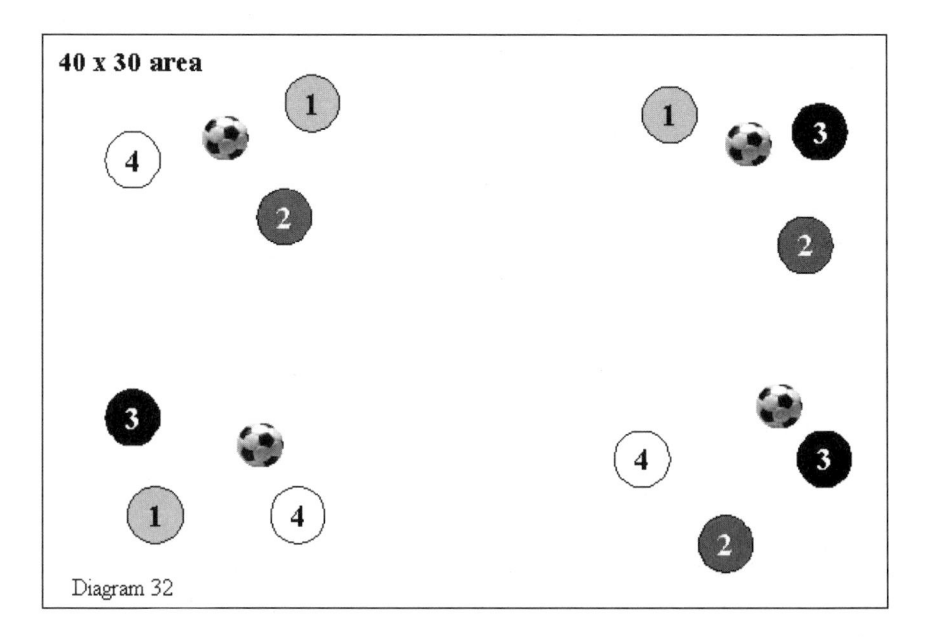

Diagram 32

These are exercises to develop movement and awareness on and off the ball. See how quickly players react to this and find their position.

A.I.A. CHANGEOVER SESSION

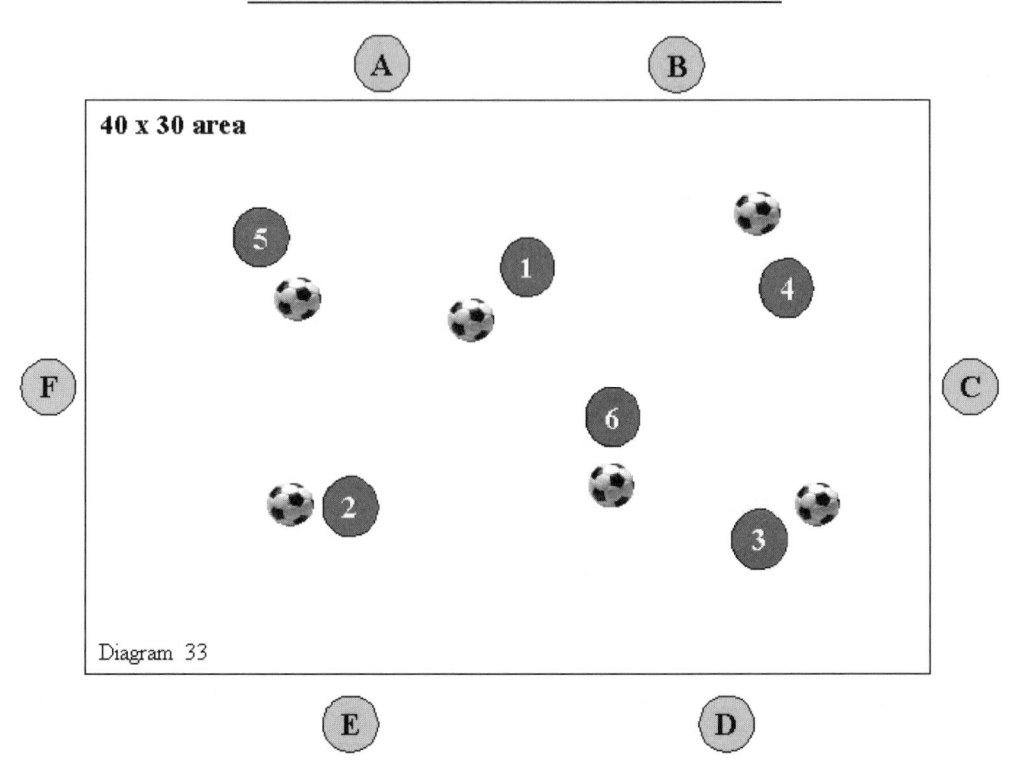

Diagram 33

1. Inside team a ball each, look to find a free outside team player and pass to them. Outside player brings the ball back in, inside player moves outside the zone waiting to receive a pass from someone else.

2. Set up second touch with a good first touch. Awareness of who is free for a pass.

3. Work on a) first touch of outside player b) decision making of inside player in terms of when and where to pass and technique (quality) of pass.

4. The Coach can create conditions:

a) Get a turn in or dribble before passing.
b) All in (many) touches, 3 then 2 touches.
c) Play 1- 2 with inside player then go outside.
d) Do a crossover with outside player rather than make a pass.

5. Inside player passes to outside player and closes down quickly, simulating a defensive movement. The receiver has to make a good first touch away from the pressure (ie to either side of the pressuring player).

6. It's a good session because everyone is working but they get short intermittent rests, so maintaining quality.

ANTICIPATION, IMAGINATION, AWARENESS

NUMBERS GAME: PASSING IN SEQUENCE

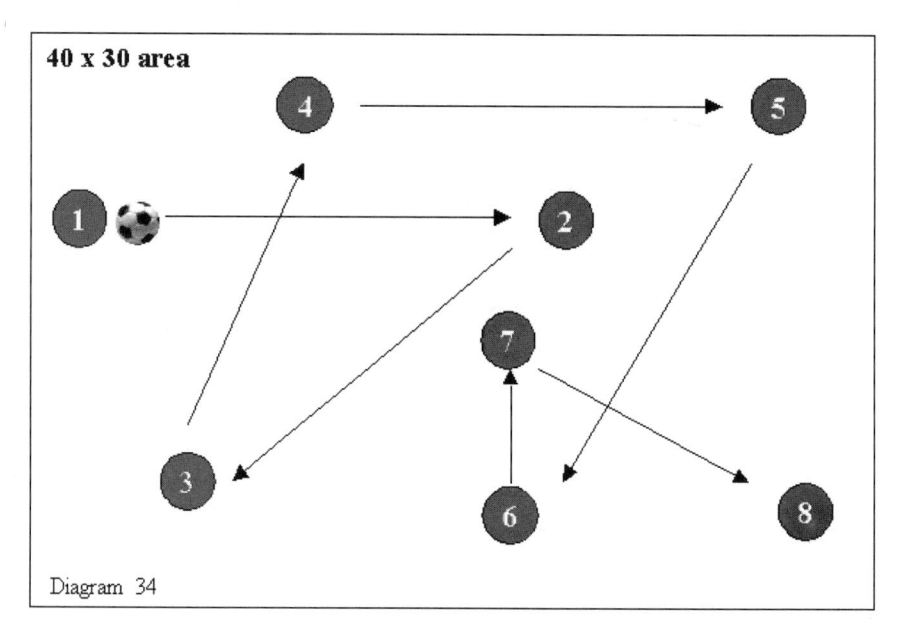

Diagram 34

1. 8 Players and only 1 ball to begin. Players must pass in sequence :
1 passes to 2; 2 passes to 3; 3 to 4 and so on to 8 who passes to 1 and we
begin again. You can have players static to begin then have them passing
and moving.

2. Player receives from the same person and passes to the same person each
time. This develops great awareness of time, space and player positions.
Continuous work on and off the ball.

3. Awareness of: where the player you receive from is and where the player you
pass to is. Because of this, players begin to anticipate the pass to them and
where it is coming from. Also they must look to where it is going (where is
the player they are passing to?).

4. We are trying to create a situation where players are looking two moves
ahead, not just one. For instance as (1) is about to pass to (2), (3) should be
looking to support (2) for the next pass, looking two moves ahead before the
ball leaves (1). Peripheral Vision Development results from this.

5. Ask players to make it difficult to find them by lots of movement off the ball to
test their teammates' vision.

6. Develop: Use two balls then three balls at the same time. Start with a ball at
(1) and (5) then at (1), (4) and (7). To keep the sequence going, players must
move the balls quickly with few touches, hence their peripheral vision development improves dramatically. As soon as they have passed one ball off, the
next one is arriving. Quick thinking is needed to make the correct decisions.

ANTICIPATION, IMAGINATION, AWARENESS

INTRODUCE ANOTHER TEAM TO THE SAME ZONE

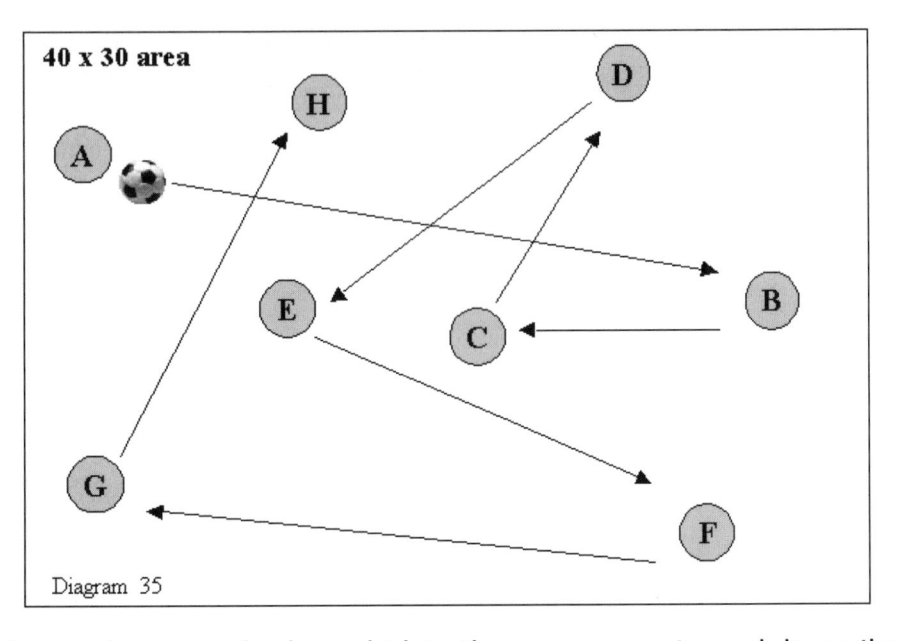

Diagram 35

The team above can be brought into the same zone to work in as the first team, each with a ball.

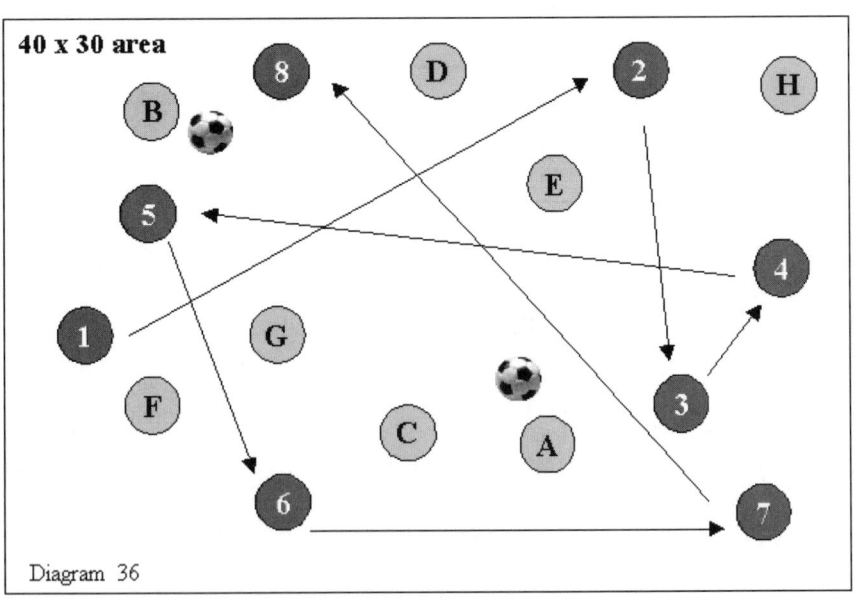

Diagram 36

You can begin with two teams in the bigger zone (combined zones of each team) and then have them play in the one zone where it's tight and more difficult to maneuver.

PASSING IN TWO'S

Two teams e.g. 6 per team, one ball for every two players. The pairs move around the zone passing their ball back and forth. Change to a ball for every three, passing and moving off each other. Then two balls per team passing to any player in that team (more choices to pass to).

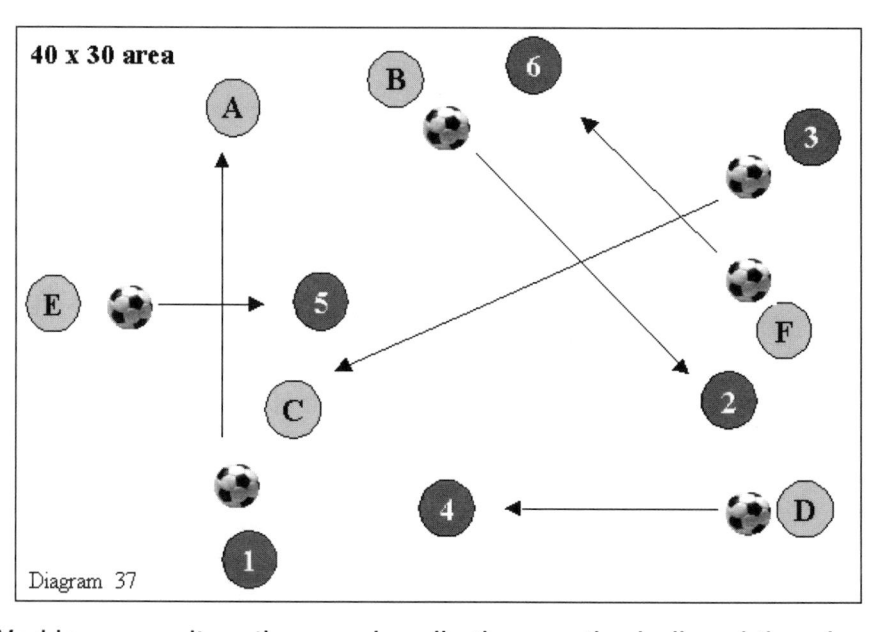

40 x 30 area

Diagram 37

1. Working opposites, the coach calls time on the ball and the players know they receive the ball when they check back (play off the second run).

2. Coach calls no time on the ball and players know they will get an early pass into their path (play off the first run).

3. This is particularly good for forward players to work on, recognizing when the player has time on the ball or not. This helps determine their movement off the ball.

4. To simulate turning and receiving to feet, (1) for example passes to his teammate then moves away to an outside line to check back to receive. Think about the angle and distance to receive and the body position (link this to coaching point number 1). When they receive the ball they keep possession until their teammate is ready to receive again after checking and turning from the line. The check away to come back is likened to when a forward runs a defender off to create space to come back into to give themselves time on the ball.

ANTICIPATION, IMAGINATION, AWARENESS

PASSING IN TRIANGLES OF THREE

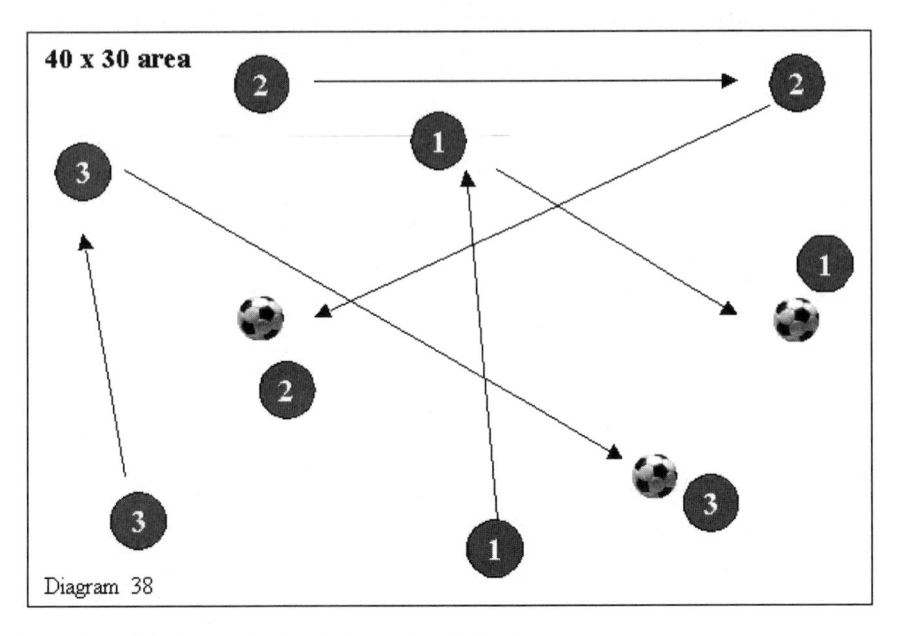

40 x 30 area

Diagram 38

1. Using the A.I.A. technical / tactical design.

2. Three or four groups of three players, each group with a ball. Players pass and move within the grid, passing through the other groups to their teammates.

3. Players must control the ball with the inside and outside of the foot moving the ball on their first touch.

4. Vary the distances of the passes, making short or long passes.

5. Runs can be coming short and spinning away to receive long into space, or running away long to come back short and receive to feet.

6. The third player moves to create a support position using the correct angle in the appropriate space to support the second player who may lay the ball off one touch and the cycle continues.

7. Previous ideas on passing in two's apply also in three's.

TRANSITION GAME
DEFENSE TO ATTACK / ATTACK TO DEFENSE

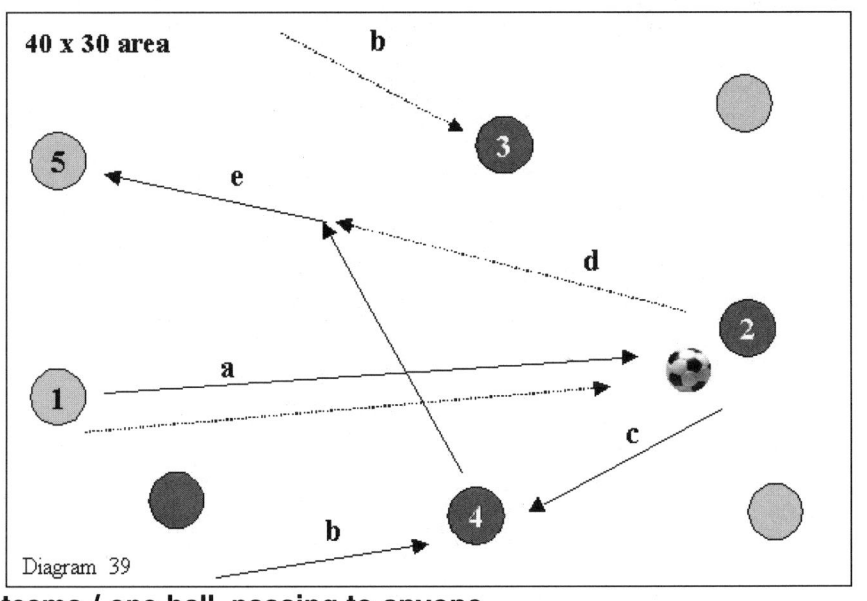

Diagram 39

Two teams / one ball, passing to anyone.

1. Passer (1) plays the ball to the receiver (2). The passer (1) then becomes a defender and must pressurize receiver (2).

2. Receiver (2) must work a 1 - 2 around the defender (1) with a support player. Try to establish support on both sides of the receiver so there are two options available to support (3 and 4).

3. Work on angles and distances of support (triangular support), timing of the pass depending on the closeness of the defender, quality of pass, preferably off the front foot to aid the disguise of the pass.

4. Receiver accepts 1 - 2 from support player (4), passes to a new receiver (5) and becomes the new defender and the cycle begins again.

5. Routine - a) 1 passes to 2 and pressurizes. b) 3 and 4 move to support 1 (thinking two moves ahead). c) 2 passes to 4. d) 2 runs around 1 to receive (give and go). e) Now 2 passes to 5 and becomes the defender.

6. Develop - Increase number of balls, passing to opposite color only but support from same color i.e. pass opposite, support same. Quick decisions required.

7. Passer plays the ball to receiver and closes down as a defender. Receiver must move the ball away first time or draw defender in and move the ball off at an angle away from the pressure.

ANTICIPATION, IMAGINATION, AWARENESS

DRIBBLING / TURNING
COMBINATION PLAYS AND FINISHING

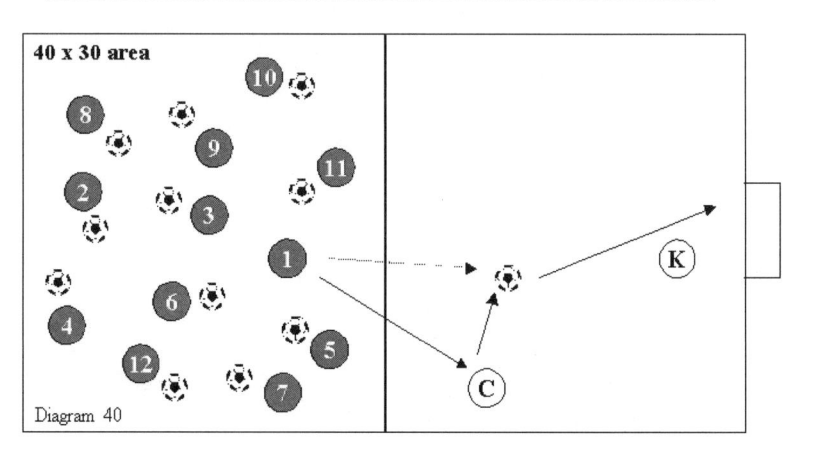

Diagram 40

1. Players can go by **number**, play a 1 - 2 with the coach and shoot or dribble around the passive defending coach. Get dribbling and control in one grid plus a shot at goal in the other.

2. **Develop** - Have a player in the coaches position who must come short to the ball to receive and turn and shoot, the passer then takes his place. Coach can be a passive defender.

3. **Defending and Attacking** - One player starts as a defender and another player with a ball must beat him and score. The shooter becomes the defender for the next one.

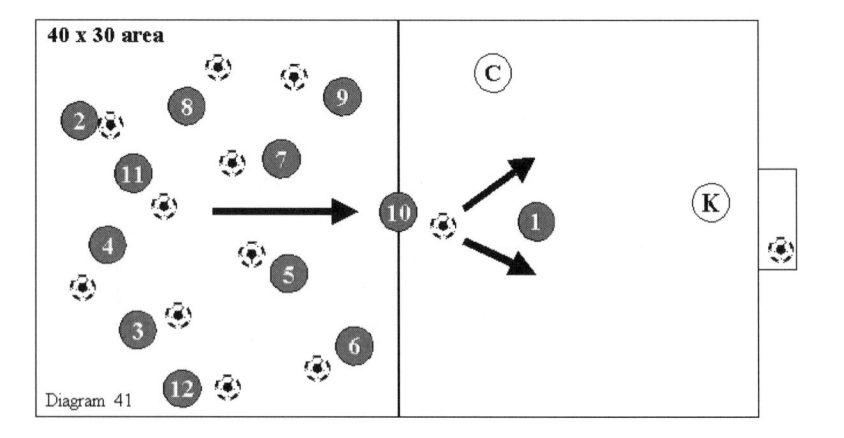

Diagram 41

COMBINATION PLAY WORKING IN TWO'S

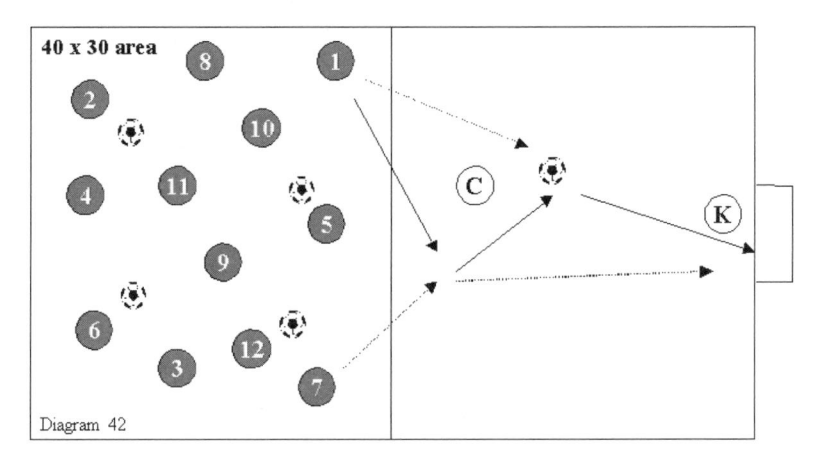

Diagram 42

1. **Combination Play (in 2's)** - Use the awareness session passing and moving. Then a player on the ball makes a decision to pass to the coach who lays it off for a supporting player without a ball to shoot (or cross if pushed too wide). Follow in for Rebounds. If two players with a ball each go, then the one who is last to go must turn back and join the group.

2. **Develop** - The coach is a passive defender; in the above example (1) plays a 1 - 2 around the coach with (7) to shoot on goal.

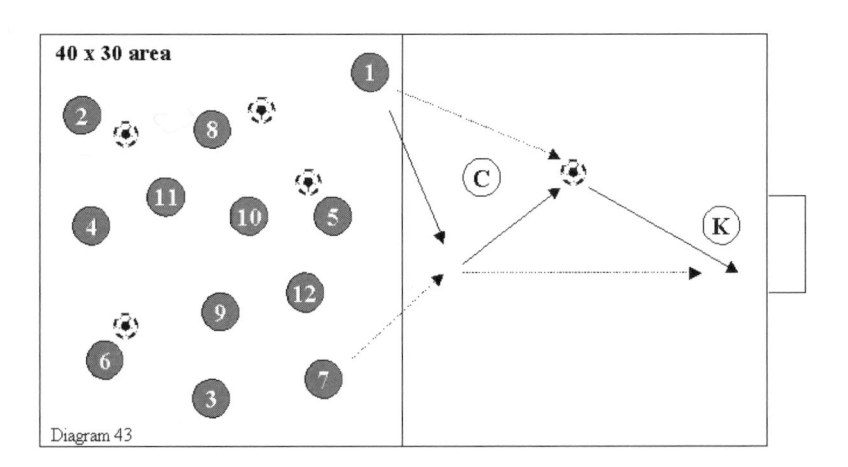

Diagram 43

COMBINATION PLAYS, DECISION MAKING
WHEN TO ATTACK

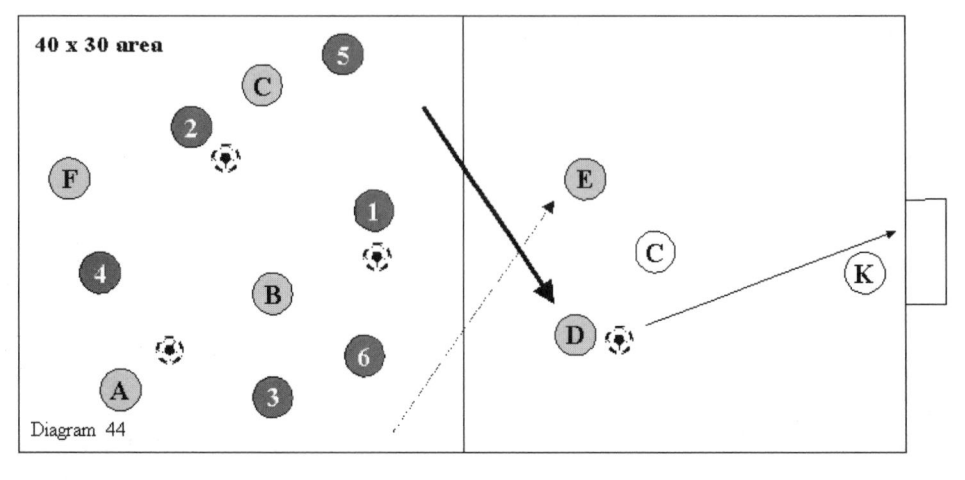

Diagram 44

1. **Two Teams** - Passing to own teammates but attacking the goal alternately (allows the shot at goal and the player to get back to the group before the same group goes again).Attacking in one's (1 - 2 with the coach or dribbling around the coach to shoot).Change by passing to the opposite team only.

2. **Combination play** - In two's (a player without a ball from the same team must support and make a 1 - 2, an overlap run , crossover or diagonal run to receive and shoot or act as a decoy).Coach acts as passive opposition. (D) Makes a diagonal run. (E) makes a diagonally opposite run. (D) can shoot and use (E) as a decoy or pass to (E) to shoot and follow in for rebounds.

3. **Develop** - Passing to opposite colors and only an opposite color can support in two's (improves peripheral vision and awareness, identifying when the break is on and who it's with).

4. All the players are constantly at work passing and moving (no standing in lines awaiting a turn) then must decide when and where to go.

5. **Coaching Points**

   a) **Passing and Support** play.
   b) **Decision** - When and where to attack.
   c) **Technique** - of the pass (timing, weight and accuracy).
   d) **Timing** of the runs.
   e) **Execution of the shot** - Accuracy and Power.

ANTICIPATION, IMAGINATION, AWARENESS

INCORPORATING CROSSING AND FINISHING

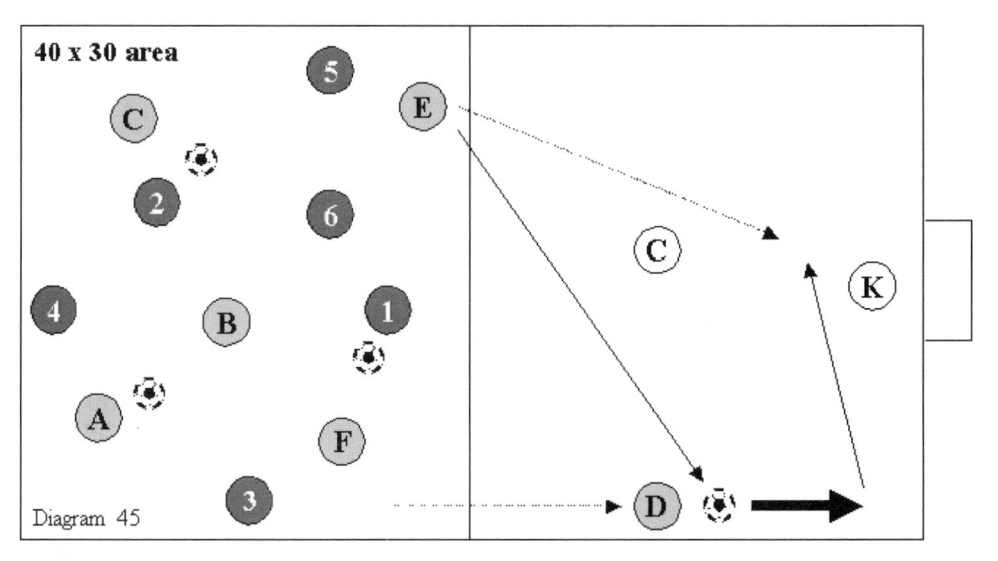

Diagram 45

1. Crossing and finishing exercise, playing a ball wide to the supporting player to receive a cross back.

2. Players are constantly working passing and moving. They must then recognize **when** and **where** to break forward in two's and attack the goal.

Coaching Points

    a) **Passing and Support** play
    b) **Decision** when and where to attack.
    c) **Technique** of the pass (timing, weight and accuracy).
    d) **Timing** of the run to receive the cross.
    e) **Angle** of the run to receive the cross.
    f) **Quality** of the cross (timing, height, pace, and direction).

3. Once two players have performed their move, they collect a ball and join back in with the group. The next two players must go through the decision making process of when to attack the goal and so on.

SPECIFIC PERIPHERAL VISION COACHING SESSION

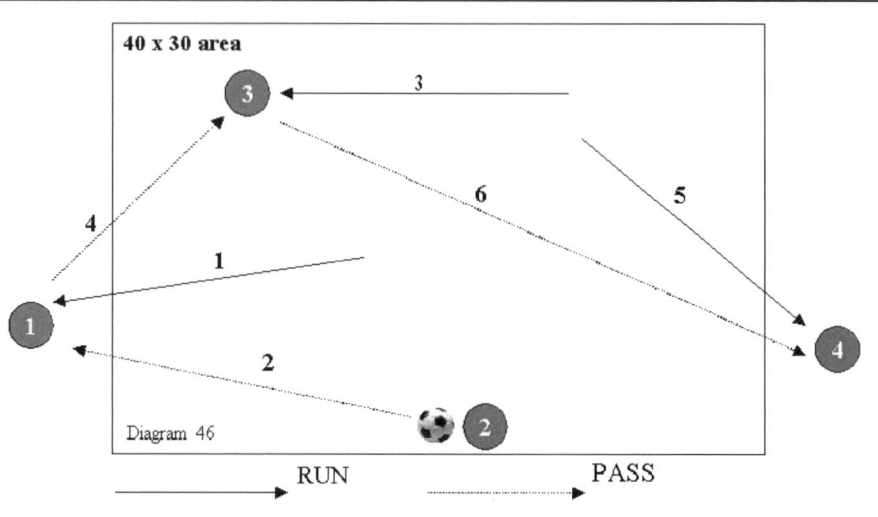

Diagram 46

RUN   PASS

This is a simplified set-up to get initial understanding. Increase numbers as previously e.g. two teams of six. We started earlier with one ball and six players for example so each person on the ball had five passing options and that was easy.

Now we must identify one and only one pass and must try to make it. That pass is to the person who runs outside the zone. This player is the free player (unmarked). The session goes as follows:

1. Player (1) runs outside the area (perhaps after several passes within the zone).

2. Player (2) on the ball sees the run and must pass to (1).

3. As (1) is about to receive (as the ball is traveling to him) (3) moves into a position to support (1) showing anticipation and awareness.

4. As (3) receives the pass, (4) makes a run out the area.

5. (3) has already seen the run by (4) and passes. (4) brings the ball back in and the game continues. This is an indicator of how quickly players recognize the run and consequently make the pass.

6. Players are beginning to look one and two moves ahead of the ball. It doesn't need to happen so quickly in terms of the next player running outside but it serves as an example. The run can be likened to a penetrating run into the attacking third where the player hasn't been picked up or tracked and is in a great position to attack and score if the passer sees him and makes that pass.

ANTICIPATION, IMAGINATION, AWARENESS

Further development, ideas and ideals of this practice leading to the introduction of defenders as opposition but in an attacking overload situation.

1. Within the zone there are many passing options, but as soon as a player makes the run outside that is the pass to make. Coach can determine the tempo of the game e.g. to avoid too many running out at the same time the coach can signal to an individual player to move out without the others knowing so only one at a time goes out.

2. Once the free player is outside and waiting for a pass, see how many passes are made inside the zone before someone sees the right pass i.e. to the outside player. This is an indication of which players play with their heads up (and hence have good peripheral vision) and which don't, (hence have poor peripheral vision or even none at all).

3. The fewer touches on the ball the player needs to get the ball there, the greater his anticipation of the run. (One touch is the ultimate aim to develop: as the ball is traveling to the player, another player makes his run out and the passer sees the run and makes the pass at the same time).

4. More touches means more reaction time needed and in a game situation this may lead to the player being caught in possession before getting around to making the pass.

5. Initially the coach may see several passes made within the area while a player stands and waits outside until someone sees him; this will happen less and less as you practice and as the players improve their peripheral vision.

6. The exciting part of this is when the coach sees one of the players make the right pass quickly in a game situation due to the work they have done in this session.

7. Up to now there have been "**NO OPPOSITION**" **GAMES**, (**SHADOW PLAYS)** to allow players to develop anticipation, awareness, vision and imagination regarding passing, receiving, support and composure on the ball. We can now start to introduce **DEFENDERS** to add pressurizing situations to test the players. Begin with the **OVERLOAD PRINCIPLE** to help gain success (e.g. 6 v 3).

SOME COMPETITIVE PRACTICES TO PROGRESS TO NON - DIRECTIONAL THREE TEAM GAME (3 v 3 v 3)

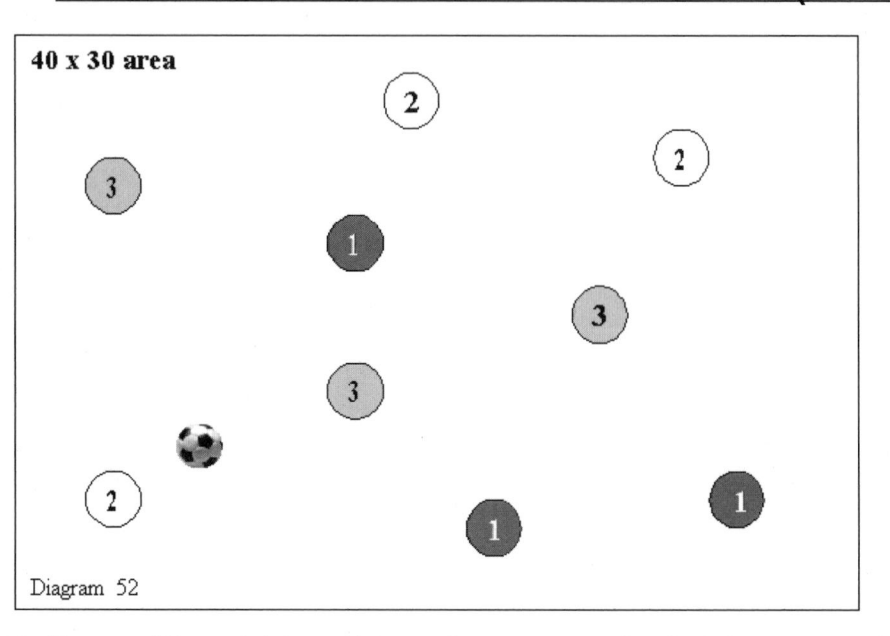

Diagram 52

1. Teams (1) and (2) work together to keep the ball from team (3). If team (3) regains possession, the team who gave it away becomes the defenders. The defenders' reward is they keep the ball and link with the other team.

2. Rules: Once possession is gained, to establish who gave the ball away the defender who won the ball puts his foot on the ball to stop play and the coach can call out the team who gave it away. Play begins again, working on transitions.

3. Develop : Increase difficulty for attackers by :

a) Reducing the zone size.
b) Decreasing the number of touches on the ball of each player.
c) Condition the passing to be only to the other attacking team's players e.g. (1) only pass to (2) and vice versa. Therefore, only half the number of passes are available per player.
d) You can increase the numbers to suit how many players you have, e.g. 4 v 4 v 4 or 5 v 5 v 5 etc.

DIRECTIONAL A.I.A. SESSION FOCUSING ON PASSING / SUPPORT AND RUNNING WITH AND WITHOUT THE BALL

LONG PASSING

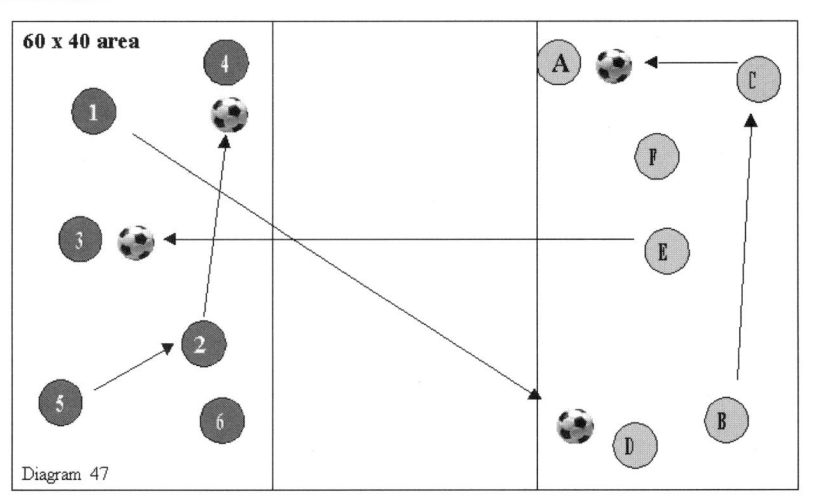

Diagram 47

1. **Pass and move** in own grid until eye contact with a player in the other grid (or a call) then play a **long pass** to that player. Balls are constantly changing grids, players have to have **awareness** in their own grid to receive but also awareness of when a pass is on from the other grid (must have head up and be constantly looking around to see this).If they don't observe where their own teammates are or those in the other grid are, they won't be successful with this so they must play with their head up and have the ability to look **away** from the ball as well as **at** it, observing all the options that are on both in their own grid and the other one.

2. **Conditions** - Ball can't bounce between grids for chipped or lofted passes, or must be driven along the ground with pace for quick passing.

3. Develop **Running with the Ball** across the grids. Pass and move within own grid, then a player picks a moment to run and takes it.

4. Keep balance of balls in each grid. Can start with one in each, then increase to two balls per grid.

5. **Long pass** then **follow** the ball (supporting the pass) into the other grid so players as well as balls are being transferred. Players must move as quickly as possible to support in the other grid.

ANTICIPATION, IMAGINATION, AWARENESS

RUNNING WITH THE BALL

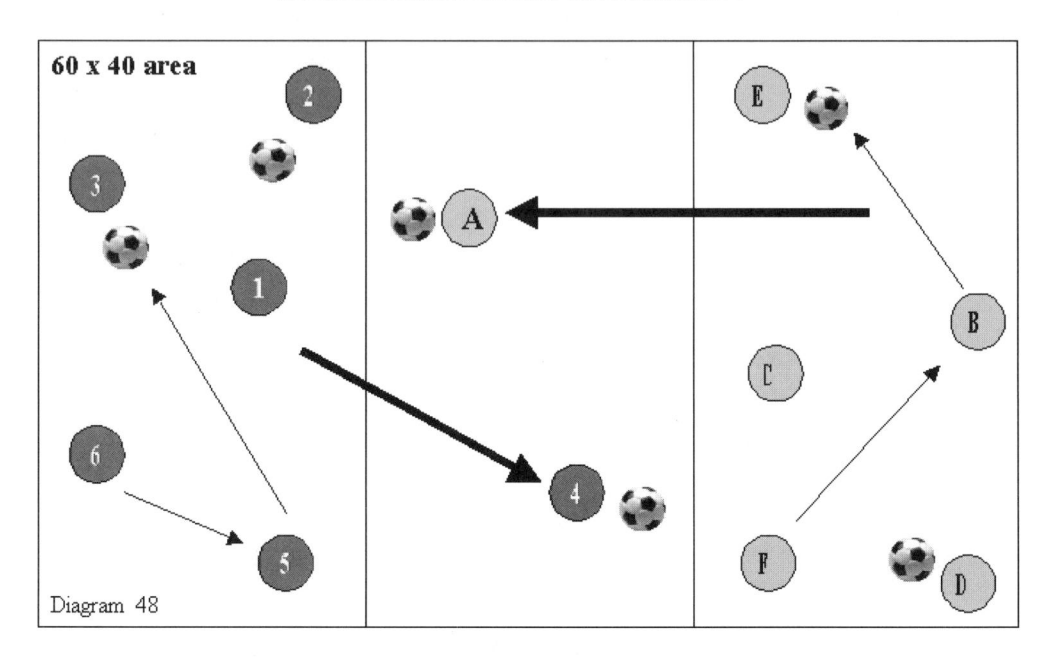

Diagram 48

PASSING THEN SUPPORTING THE PASS

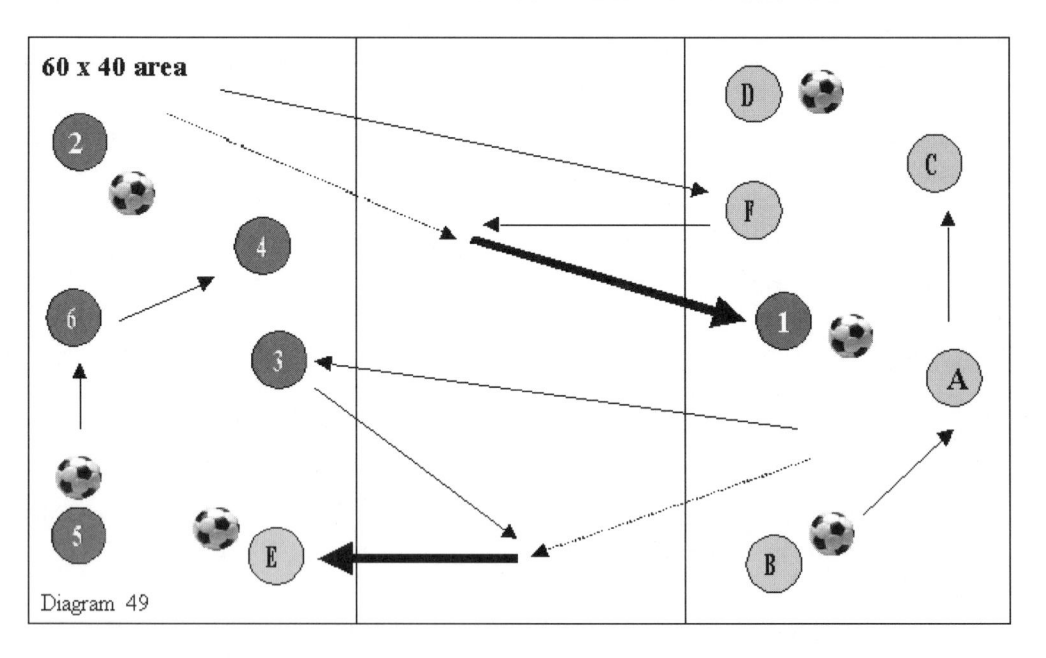

Diagram 49

6. **Third man run development** - a player makes a run into the neutral area between the grids. A player on the ball must see this quickly and pass to the player making the run. Try to drop the ball in front of the receiver to run on to. Running player then takes ball into other grid and at the same time another player goes the opposite way. Start with one ball in each grid and build up.

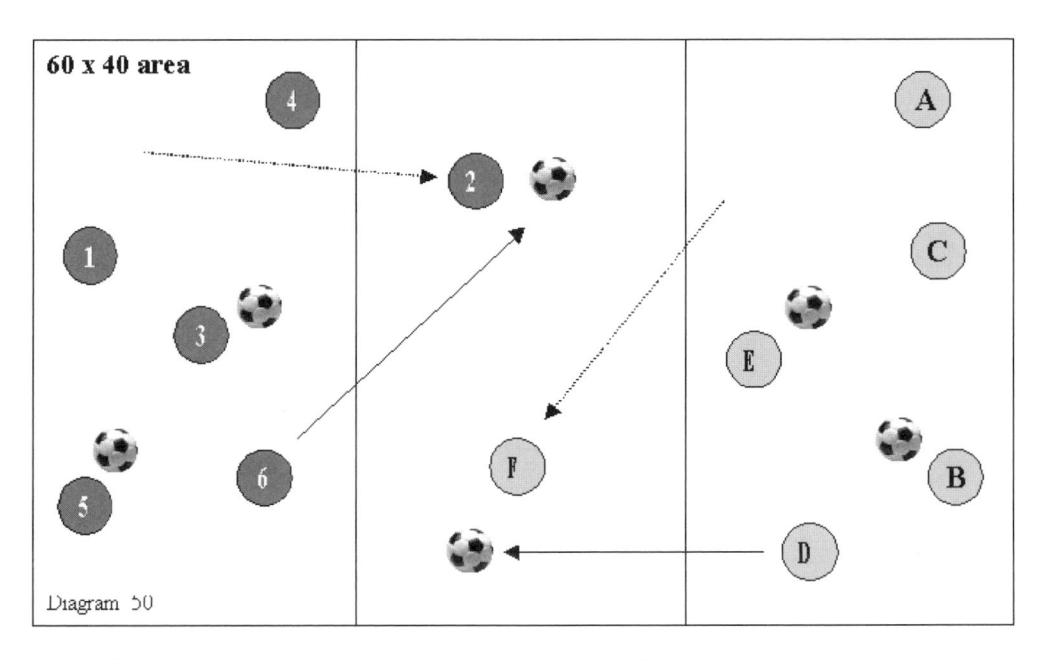

Diagram 50

7. **Develop** - the type of runs to be made, straight or diagonal runs. Diagonal passes and straight runs, and diagonal runs and straight passes as above or diagonal runs and diagonal passes. Equate the situation with how to make it difficult for defenders in a game to mark players who make different types of runs.

8. If a player makes a run and doesn't receive a pass then he works his way back into his own grid. Relate the move to a player making a forward run who doesn't get the pass, works back, drawing a defender with him and then another player makes the run into the space created to receive a through ball.

9. **Receiving and Turning** - a player moves out of the area and positions side on at an angle to receive and turn (looking before receiving) and take the ball to the other grid. Same happens on the other side.

PLAYING GIVE AND GO'S

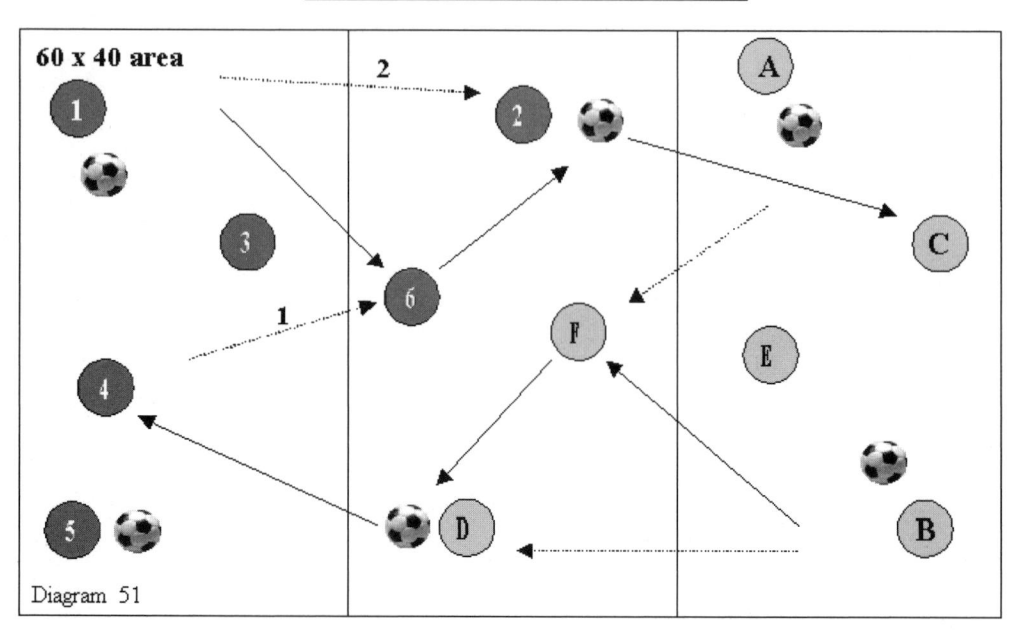

Diagram 51

10. **Give and Go's** (Movement in two's) - A player moves into the neutral zone (with a third man run off the ball) and another player on the ball passes to him. The passer then follows and receives a return pass (a 1- 2 move) and passes the ball into the other grid. Both players move into the other grid and join in. On entering, the existing players in this grid must balance things up and look to break in twos the other way as soon as possible.

11. Introduce a defender in each grid. 4 v 1, only one ball per grid.

12. As the number of players involved increases, increase the number of balls used so at times two players can be making moves across the free space from the same grid at the same time. This ensures constant movement between grids. Build up to a ratio of one ball to two players per grid as the players get good at passing and moving and being able to look beyond the ball while at the same time making quick decisions.

USING GOALS AS A SUPPORT REFERENCE

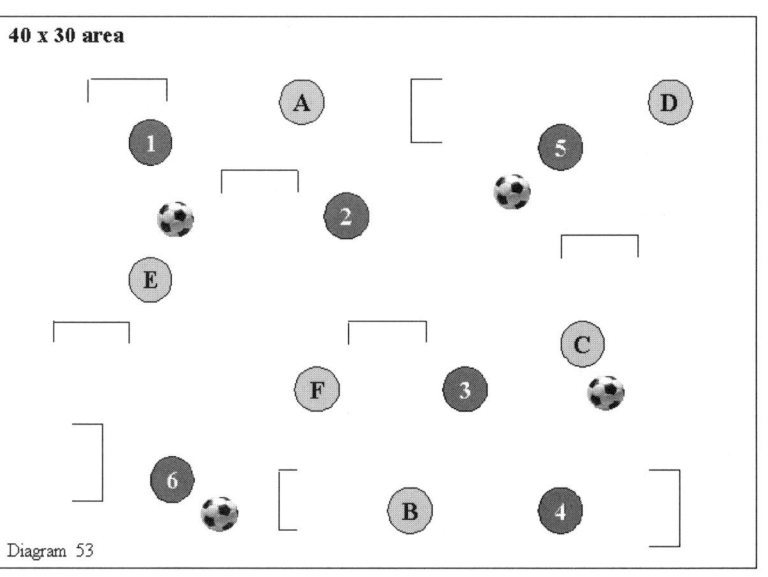

Diagram 53

1. The goals are spread out and act as a reference to help the players spread out, switch play, pass and support each other.

2. They must make their passes through the goal. This condition forces the players to find a goal (and space) to pass and to receive through. Once they receive the ball they must then find someone else to pass to. The support players spread out to receive by moving into space (where the other goals are).

3. Two teams working in the same area means congestion, so decisions have to be quick on where, when and how to pass and receive.

4. Move into an overload situation so there is opposition to increase the pressure on the players. Have an 8 v 4 in the above workout, still using the goals as points of reference for support positions. Count the number of passes made through the goals. **Develop** - score a goal by dribbling through the goal also.

5. Eventually have equal sides and make it competitive, counting passes through the goals as a goal and perhaps have the first team to ten goals be the winner. All your previous work trying to teach the players how to play in less pressurized situations (over a long period of time) to relax them, ultimately leads to you testing them in full scale match play. The progression to this must be gradual.

DIRECTIONAL FOUR GOAL SWITCHING PLAY SESSION

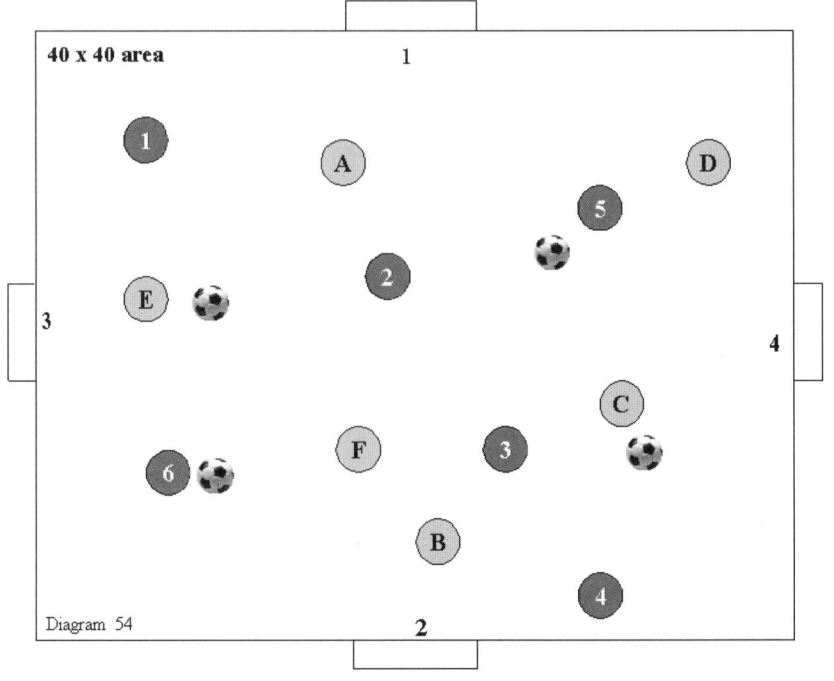

Diagram 54

1. Two teams passing and moving with a ball each team. Initially have one team attacking goal (1) and the other team goal (2). Coach calls "**switch**" and they attack different goals. **Develop** - Numbers team tries to score in goal (1) then (2) . Letters team tries to score in goal (3) then (4). Teams always play through each other but in different directions. Next, each team can attack two goals (opposite goals) at once.

2. Looking to switch play attacking two goals, players decide when to switch the ball, and which goal to attack. Have a one or two touch shooting condition so the timing of the passing and the timing of the movement into position to shoot are correct.

3. **Develop a)** Use two balls per team so they can attack two goals at once if necessary. **b)** Introduce goalkeepers in each of the four goals to make it more competitive. Have a constant supply of balls to keep the game moving.

4. Look to include all the main coaching points in the A.I.A. session. Call "**switch**" as they are playing so they attack the opposite two goals. Developing quick thinking decision-makers. Ultimately have a **competitive game** between the two teams using the various rules and conditions above.

ANTICIPATION, IMAGINATION, AWARENESS

SWITCHING PLAY GAME ENCOURAGING USING WIDTH

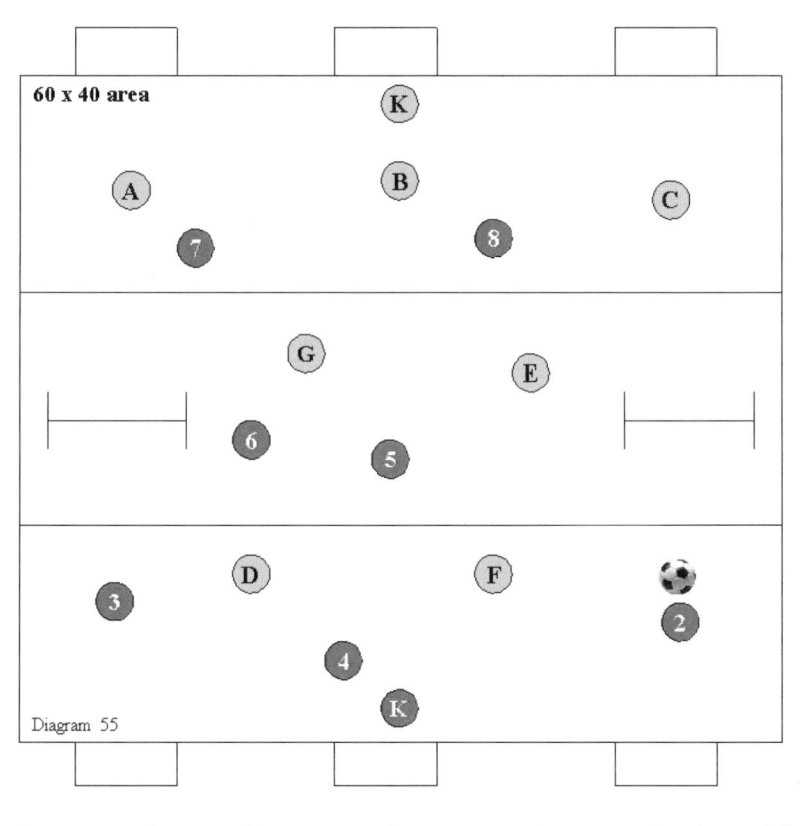

Diagram 55

1. Using three goals as reference points, award one point / goal for scoring in the central goal and two points / goals when scoring in the wide goals. This should encourage them to spread the play using width in attack. If it is tight down one side, encourage players to switch the play and go down the other side.

2. Using the goals on the field, award a point / goal if they play through the goal, again encouraging using width in attack. They can dribble or pass through these goals. What you hope for is that if it is tight down one side and they can't score because the other team is defending well, a player may spread out to the other side to receive the ball with the idea that the team can score a point / goal by passing or dribbling through the other goal on the far side of the field (thus switching the play).

SWITCHING PLAY:
FOUR SESSIONS IN ONE WITH PROGRESSIONS

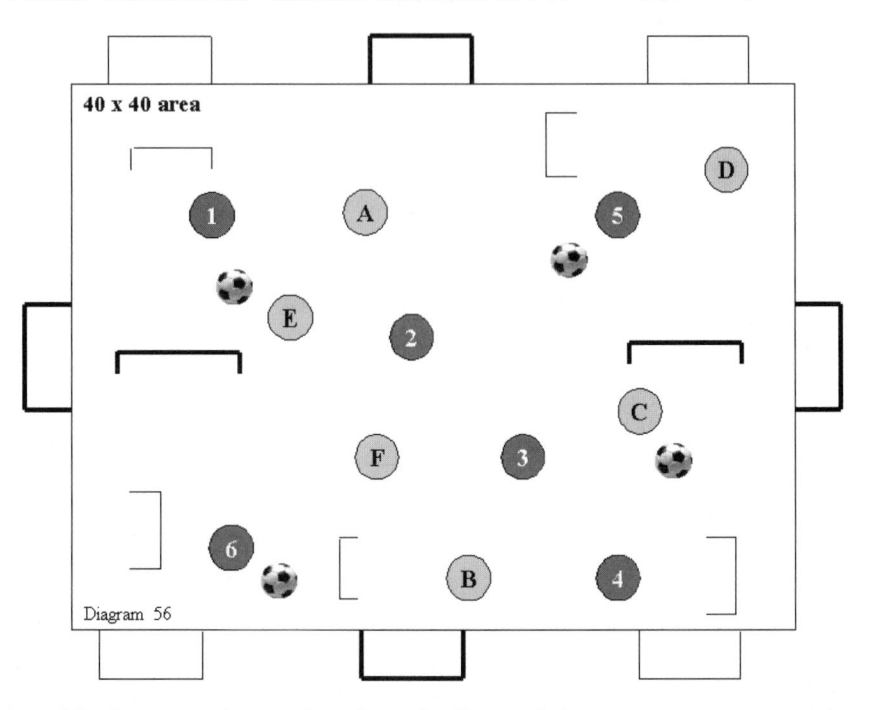

40 x 40 area

Diagram 56

1. Begin with the session using four balls and the awareness session to introduce the idea of switching play and spreading out. No opposition, just two teams playing through each other using the other team as non- competitive opposition.

2. Once this has been practiced, make it competitive with two teams competing against each other with one ball only.

3. Have the three-goal game with one point for a goal in the central goal and two for goals in the wide goals. Leave two goals inside the grid, when they pass or dribble through it they get a point.

4. Finish with a switching game using the four central goals on the four sides of the grid. Teams score in opposite goals so there are two goals to attack.

5. All the sessions are designed to help players learn how to switch the play.

SWITCHING PLAY AS A TEAM

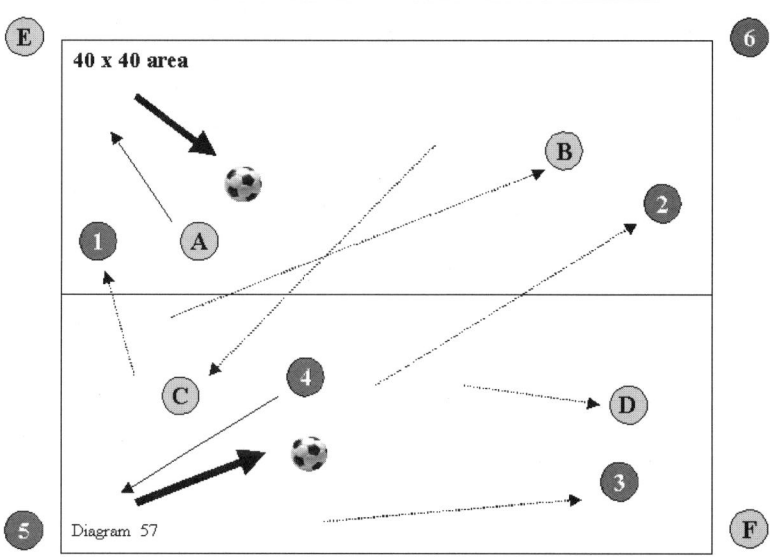

40 x 40 area

Diagram 57

1. Two teams with a ball each playing to targets. Once they get to one target they must work to get the ball to the other target. As the player passes to a target he must change over with the target player who comes into play. As above (4) passes to (5) and switches position, already the other players have spread out to attack the other target.

2. Teams play through each other and must have awareness of where their own players are and where the other team is as they pass through them. Emphasize a good first touch to set up the next pass or passing first time to a teammate. Players must look before they receive the ball.

3. Ensure as the ball is transferred from one end to the other that all players get a touch on the ball before it gets to the next target.

4. As the ball is passed to the target and the target player brings the ball out with a good first touch, the other players must already be positioning themselves to be in support to transfer the ball to the other target. This means spreading out width wise and length wise to make themselves hard to mark as in a game. Ensure they don't turn their backs and run away but keep looking at the ball and open their stance to receive a pass or at least offer an option. Show movement across the field as they break out, diagonal runs for example (C & B), no breaking in straight lines which makes them easy to mark.

5. Introduce opposition so the two teams play against each other and make it competitive by keeping score.

PASSING AND SUPPORT DIRECTIONAL TARGET GAME

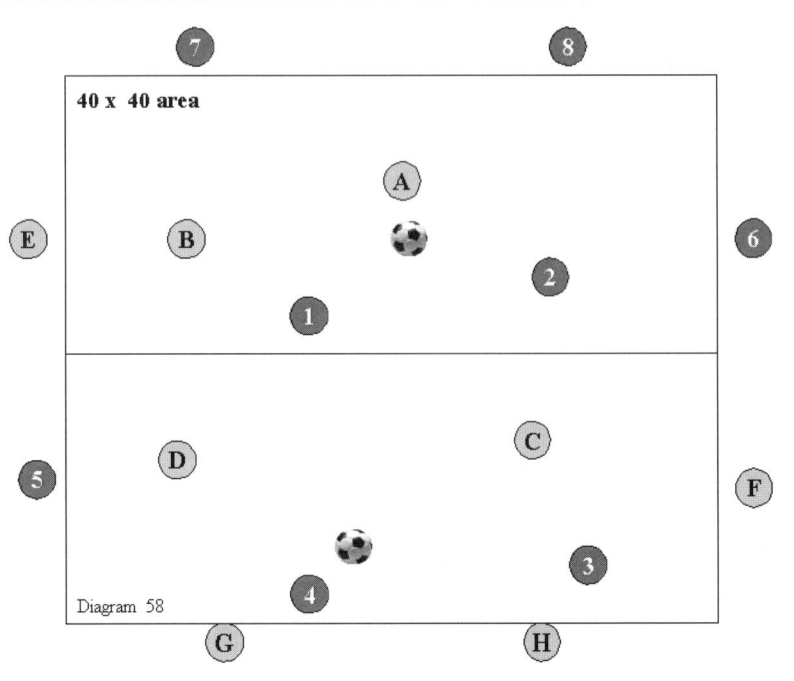

40 x 40 area

Diagram 58

1. Start with two balls and two teams passing and playing through each other, **no opposition**. Develop by having two balls per team. Have the players play in a relaxed composed way to begin. Develop into a **competitive game**.

2. This is a 4 v 4 target game (you can vary the number of players). Players must get the ball to their own end targets. If they do they retain possession as a reward. Before they can go back to a target they must pass the ball back into their **own half** of the field. Targets have two touches and can pass to any of the four players. Players can use support on the outside (1 or 2 touch). Inside players no touch restriction.

3. This is an intensive workout with little rest. Keep it short so players perform with **quality** and rotate outside players in. If a team wins the ball back in their attacking half they can go **direct** to their targets (same as regaining the ball in the attacking half and shooting for goal).

4. **Observe the Attacking Team** -Recognize their movement off the ball. For example, to work the ball into their own half, see if the players make runs early as soon as the ball is at a target. Some should support short and some long so the target has choices.

5. **Observe the Defending Team** - see if they are sucked to the ball or they recognize runs off the ball and track players making runs away from the ball into the other half.

ANTICIPATION, IMAGINATION, AWARENESS

ELEMENTS OF PLAY THE TARGET GAME TEACHES.

1. Attacking as a Team and as Individuals.

    a) Creating Space by running off the ball to receive or to help a team-mate receive.

    b) Developing quick support play, working angles and distances by incorporating switching play using the side players.

    c) Passing long and short to targets and to teammates.

    d) Receiving and turning in tight situations and dribbling in 1 v 1 situations.

    e) Lots of touches on the ball for the players in this practice.

    f) Quick decision making is required in this session because the numbers are small, the area tight and the transitions rapid.

2. Defending as a Team and as Individuals.

    a) Pressurizing players on the ball to regain possession.

    b) Supporting pressuring players and tracking runners off the ball.

    c) High pressure to regain possession in the attacking half to be able to go straight to the target to score.

3. Transitions from defense to attack and attack to defense, quick decision-making and improved concentration as the switch occurs. Interchanges of positions between inside players, targets and side support players.

4. As a coach you can work in this session how to defend properly as individuals and a team or how to attack properly both individually and as a team.

CONDITIONS TO CHANGE THE FOCUS OF THE GAME

1. No restriction on touches, then three, two or one touch, but only if it is appropriate to do so.

2. Introduce neutral player so there is a 5 v 4 overload in the middle if possession isn't kept easily.

3. Interchanges of players outside to in, inside to out as they pass the ball. Observe the quality of the pass and the first touch of the receiver.

4. Have one teammate at each end so you are **attacking both ends,** but once you have passed to one target you keep possession and must try to get to the other target. You can't go back unless the opposition wins the ball and you get it back. Only then can you go back to the same target.

5. To lessen the workload and keep everyone involved, have players switch with targets and outside players when they pass to them. This causes a constant transition of players and focuses the players' concentration.

6. The team can only score if they get an **overlap, crossover or 1 - 2** in during the build up.

7. No talking, so players have to rely on their own vision to play.

8. Players move into the target zone to receive (timing of run and pass) so we don't play with set targets. Different players can then become the target player.

9. Man - Marking - Have the players man mark so they must track a player when they don't have the ball and must lose their marker when they have the ball. This is a good test to see who is working hard and who isn't, as they have a designated job to do. You as a coach can see who works to get free of his marker and who works hard to prevent the player he is marking from getting the ball.

QUICK TRANSITION PLAY
ENCOURAGING DRIBBLING AND TURNING

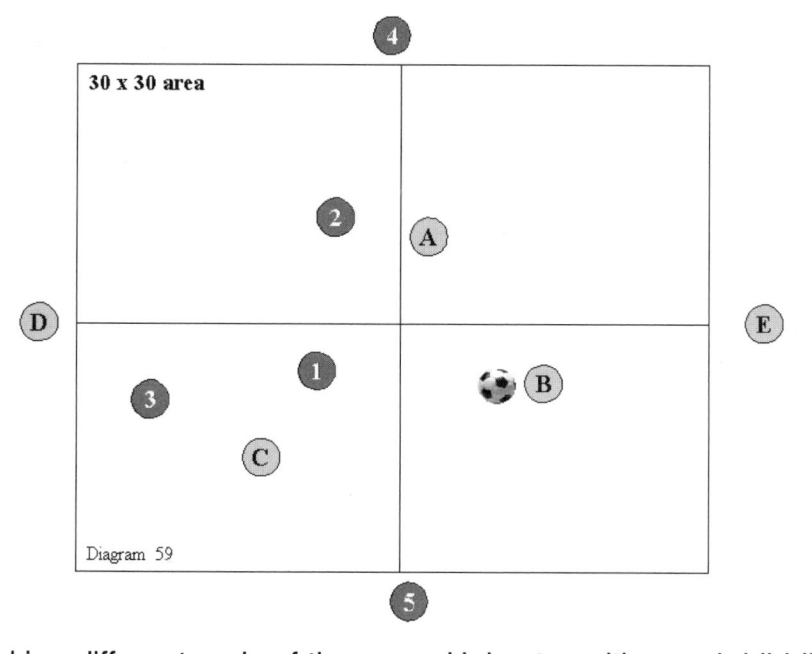

Diagram 59

1. Attacking different ends of the zone. Helps transition and dribbling and turning on the ball (a goal is scored by passing the ball to a target and keeping possession).

2. Outside players change with inside players who pass to them. Attack the opposite target.

3. A player must be up to the half way line to score. This encourages dribbling and running with the ball.

4. Players get a rest by passing into the target and transitioning positions. This maintains quick quality play because players don't get too tired (quality drops because of fatigue).

5. Small zone to work in, resulting in lots of goals, reinforcing success.

Coaching Points

a) Players must change direction as they gain possession of the ball because they are defending one end then suddenly attacking at right angles to where they were defending. Aids quick decision-making.

b) Attitude to attack quickly is important so players must be positive in mind and action.

c) Individual 1 v 1's and team passing and support play. Everything should be done at pace.

d) Quality of pass by inside player, quality of first touch by outside player to move into space quickly and set up a new attack.

QUICK TRANSITION DIRECTIONAL PLAY

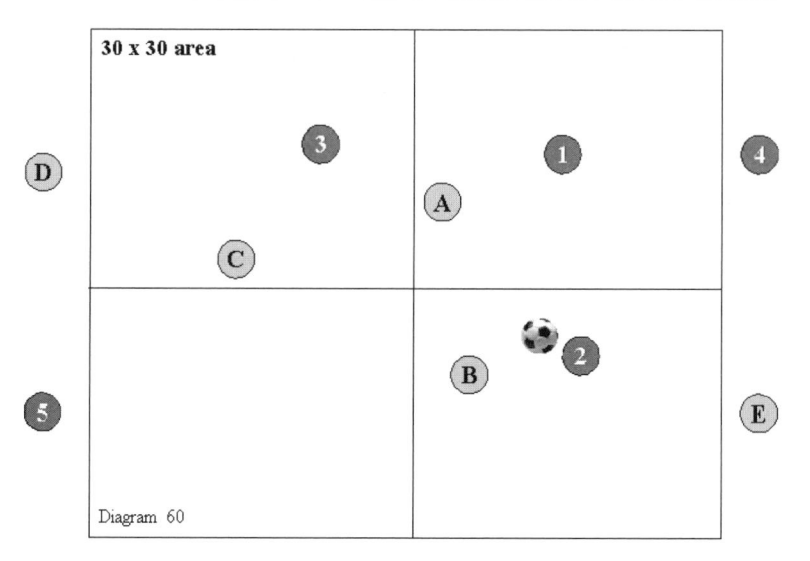

Diagram 60

1. Quick continuous attacking play which is good for anaerobic fitness. Breaking one way, passing to an outside player and switching positions, inside player out, outside player in, then attack the other side of the zone.

Coaching Points

a) Technical ability on the ball in 1 v 1 situations.

b) Quick Transition in attack - As the transition between players happens (for example (3) changes with (5)), the numbers team must get the ball to (4) as quickly as possible.

c) Observe the movement of (2) and (1) in terms of their support positions as the directional change takes place. They must move in anticipation to find space to help the player on the ball as the switch occurs.

d) Observe also, as the change occurs, the positions of the defending team. Has the decision on who presses the ball been made quickly enough? Are the other defensive players supporting and covering and especially tracking runners off the ball? The coach must learn to look away from the ball and observe what may happen next before it happens.

e) This session improves quick decision making and tight control because of the limited space, and thinking in advance due to the switch in direction of the play. You can also work on the defending players.

PRESSURIZING GAME WORKING ON TRANSITIONS

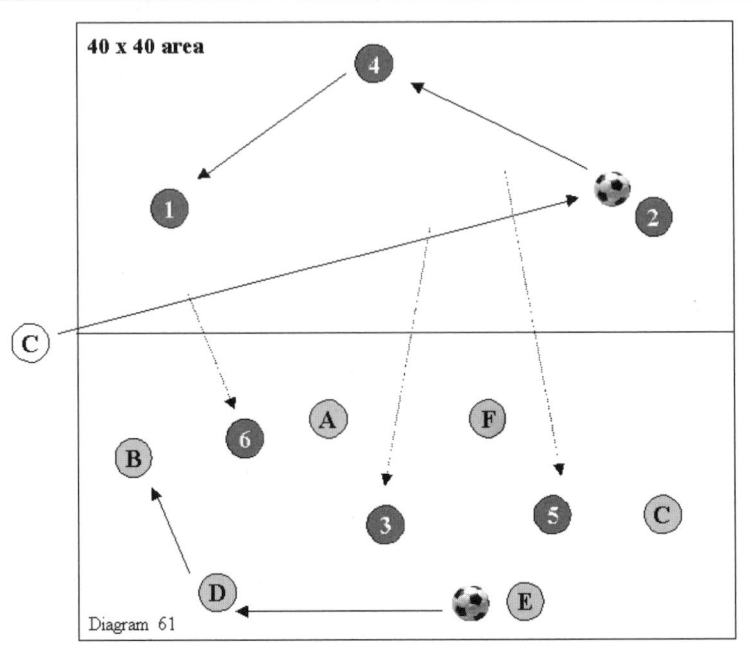

Diagram 61

1. A **Transition game** creating 6 v 3 situations in both halves. If the three defenders win the ball back, they work it back to their own half of the field. They then move back into their own half and three defenders from the other team go in to try to win it back (another 6 v 3).

2. While this is going on the three players left alone have a ball to pass to each other to keep them working, passing and moving until their teammates win the ball back. They then pass the ball to the coach who gives it to the remaining three players from the other team. This is using the A.I.A. principles, at all times focusing on what is happening **on the ball** and what is happening **away from the ball** and so on.

3. This also keeps the three players left from standing still or just standing close to the half way line where, if they receive the ball, the other team won't have far to run to win it back. Even without the second ball, these players should be spread out away from the action to give themselves time and space to receive the ball and keep it.

4. All players are working all the time. The three players must observe what is happening in the other half while passing their own ball around so that when their teammates win possession and bring it back into their own half they are ready to receive and also they recognize the time to play their own ball to the coach.

ANTICIPATION, IMAGINATION, AWARENESS

NUMBERS GAME INTRODUCING TEAM SHAPE IDEAS

BASIC SET-UP

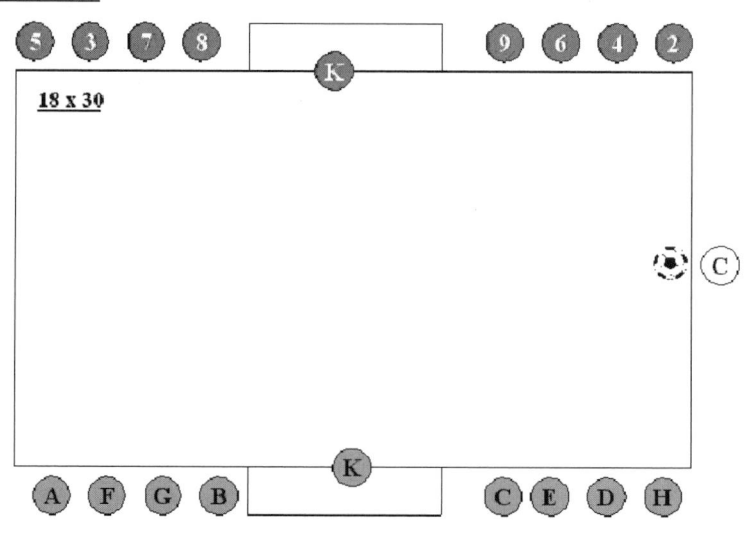

1. Two teams of 9 v 9 (it can be any number) and the coach calls a number or numbers to create two teams who play against each other.

2. The ball is played into the playing area and it is the first team to get there who gets possession and attacks. The defending team must win it back to try to score.

3. Keep score to make it competitive for the players.

4. Vary the numbers who go into the playing area. You can add them as you go e.g. do 1 v 1 then bring in another two players each team to go 3 v 3 as the game is developing.

5. As the numbers are called the teams must form a shape quickly. It can be 1 v 1 then 2 v 2 making combination plays, then 3 v 3 setting up in a triangle, then 4 v 4 in a diamond, then 5 v 5 in a 2 - 1 - 2 shape or 2 - 2 - 1, 6 v 6 in a 3 - 1 - 2 and so on.

6. When defending, the triangle or diamond is smaller (shorter and tighter) than the attacking triangle or diamond (wider and longer).

7. Monitor how quickly the teams set up their shapes to attack or defend depending on how quickly they get to the ball. The theme is scoring as quickly and efficiently as possible.

8. Finish with all the players in this area and play balls in with pace to see if they can deflect balls into the goal to score or finish 1 touch. Players can build up play also but must shoot on every occasion.

ANTICIPATION, IMAGINATION, AWARENESS

68

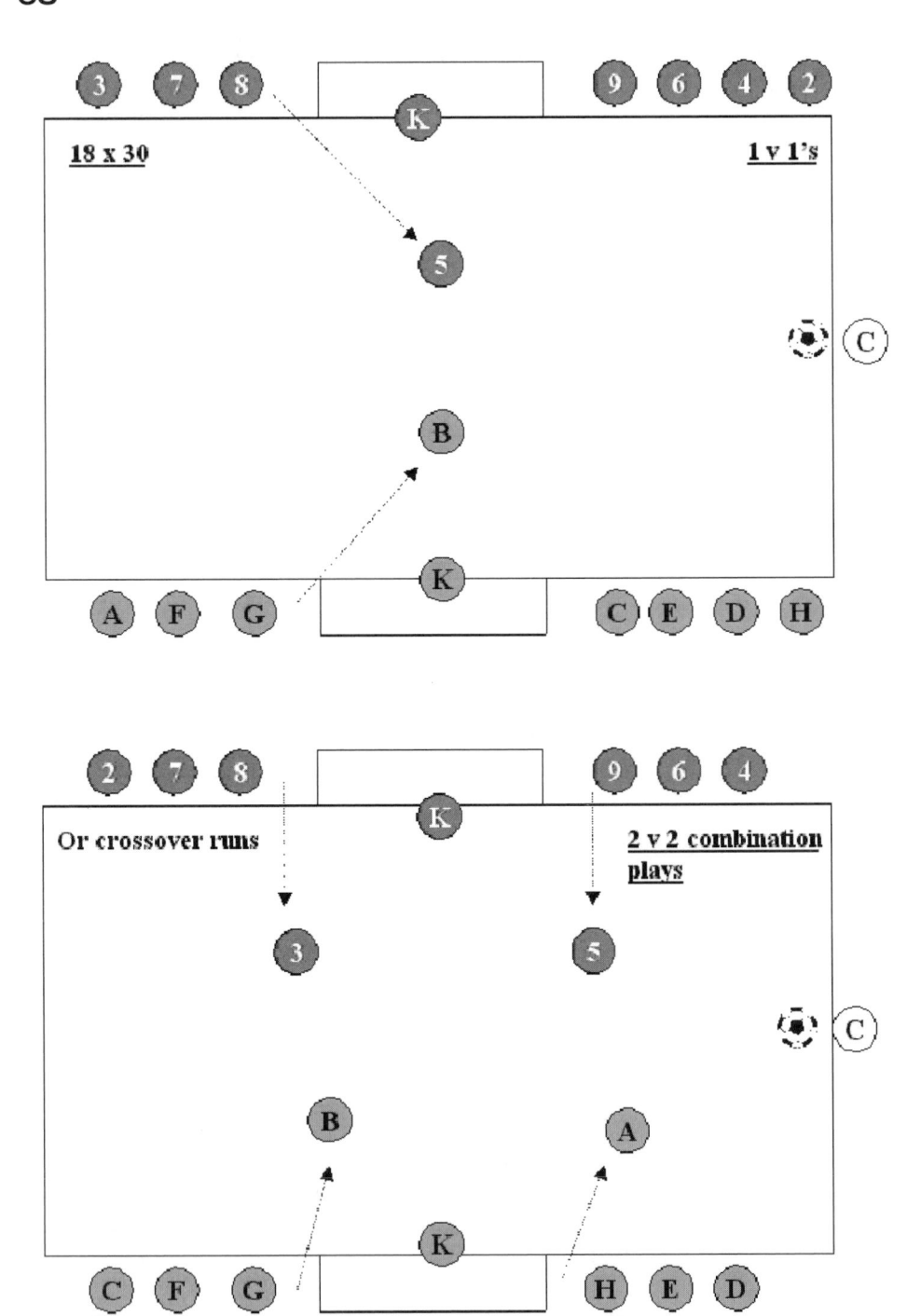

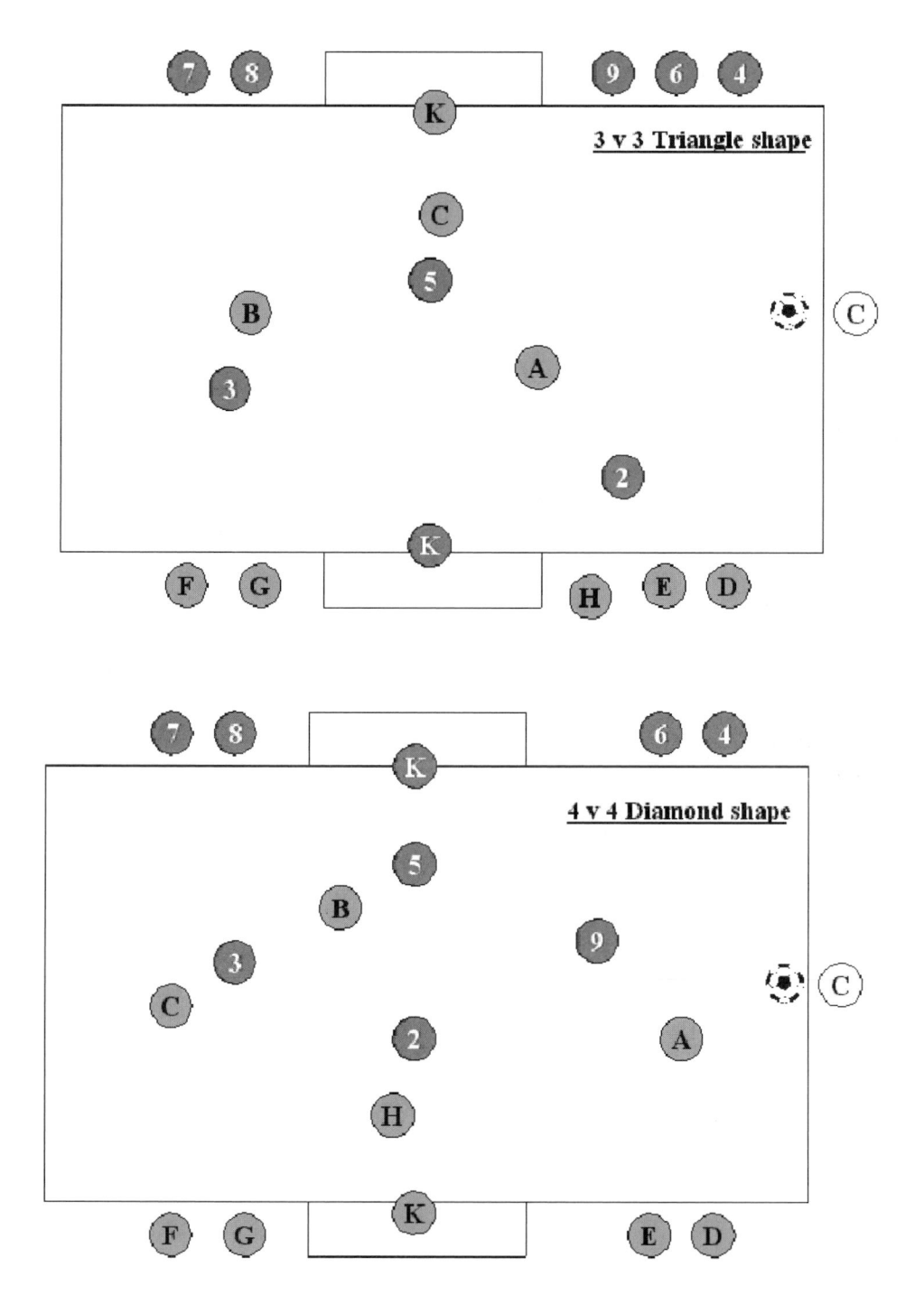

3 v 3 Triangle shape

4 v 4 Diamond shape

SMALL SIDED GAME DEVELOPMENT

In considering the development of the A.I.A. coaching program, I felt a need to relate it's use in producing soccer players to the small sided game (S.S.G) concept which in itself is an important part of player development. The two go hand in hand.

With this in mind I have produced some small sided game practices that you the coach can use to further develop the work you have already done. I have taken the S.S.G. concept from a 3 v 3 triangular set up to a 4 v 4 diamond set up through 5 v 5, 6 v 6, 8 v 8, 9 v 9 up to 11 v 11 and the full field.

To explain why 11 v 11, I would say that within a full size game of soccer there are always S.S.G. situations with combination plays occurring all over the field and by practicing with smaller numbers you are reproducing what is happening in the full game.

The difference is that in the S.S.G's it is the same small number of players involved and hence they each have a lot more touches on the ball. In the full size game, many different players are involved in many different S.S.G. situations.

Aside from the game situations, in training, coaches often have different numbers of players available to train on any one occasion. Therefore, I considered that it would be useful to show how to develop practices using different small sided game sizes in terms of player numbers and sizes of area used.

Ultimately, as the S.S.G. concept becomes more accepted and certain sized teams play officially at certain age groups, coaches can tailor their practices to suit the format their players play in from both a technical and a tactical standpoint.

8 v 8 is already played at the Under 9 and Under 10 level, 6 v 6 is being introduced at these age groups at a later date in the State of Minnesota (where I live) and I hope to see 4 v 4 games being developed in the future for the very young.

Considering all these points, providing S.S.G. practices covering different themes is an important way to aid the development of all players who are trained this way. Coaches can themselves develop these themes and can use and relate them to different team sizes from the information they get from this book. The only thing restricting them is their own imagination!!!

SMALL SIDED GAME PRACTICES

3 v 3 (INTRODUCING KEEPERS)
BASIC TRIANGULAR SHAPE

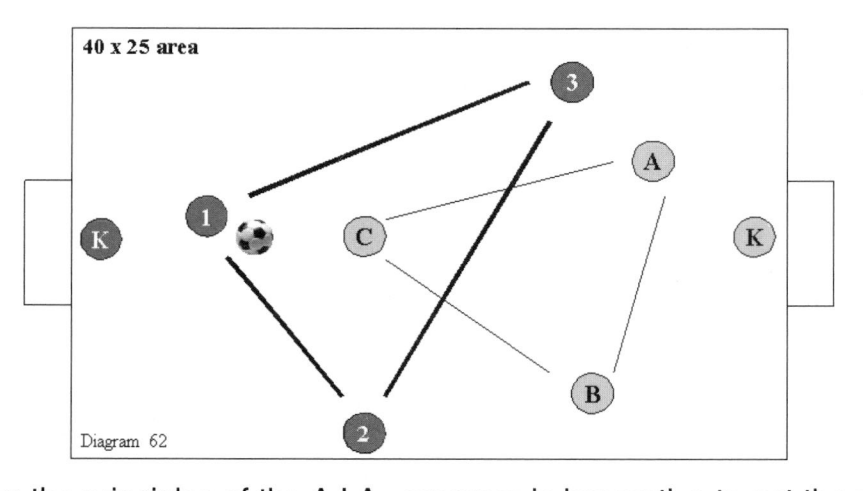

40 x 25 area

Diagram 62

1. Using the principles of the A.I.A., program is imperative to get the most success out of this small sided game concept (refer to section 4, key points checklist).

2. The 3 v 3 small sided game concept is the perfect introduction to learning triangular support shape in terms of angles and distances and establishing the supporting positions of the players.

3. Playing **3 v 3 without keepers** provides an opportunity to develop the **keeper-sweeper** concept. One player is both the keeper and the supporting defender, able to handle the ball close to the goal and use his feet away from the goal (you can have a designated area if you like, within which they can handle the ball).

4. Avoid the situation where a player from each team stays back in goal. Encourage them to get involved in open play.

5. Move to 3 v 3 plus keepers as a natural progression when the time is right. Having three permanent outfield players provides the players with more options on the field of play.

4 v 4 (OR 5 v 5 WITH KEEPERS)
BASIC DIAMOND SHAPE

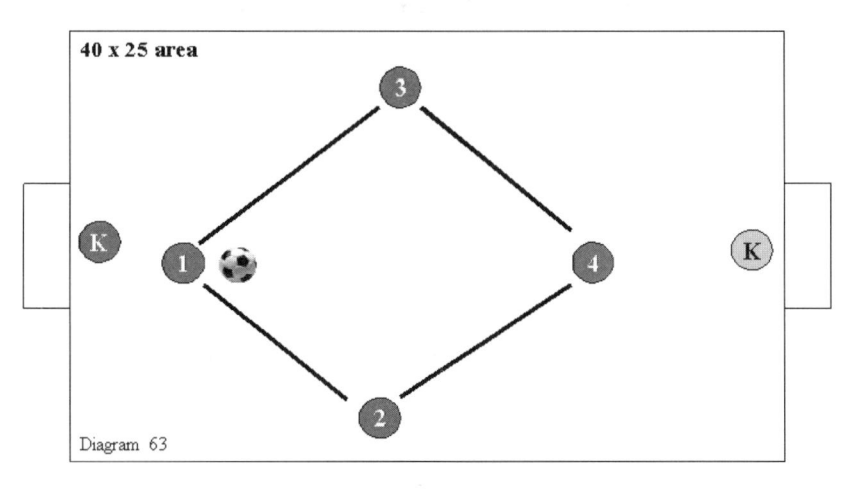

Diagram 63

1. There are no set positions but there is a **positional theme** to work from which is the **diamond or kite**. Begin with one team working up and down to each target alternately taking shape from this. Introduce another team and have them playing through each other.

2. You can have two keepers in goal (or coaches) as targets to pass to, then players **reverse their direction** of play attacking the opposite goal. Keep it continuous, using the other team as non-competitive opponents to play through.

3. The coach can introduce **combination plays** for the players to practice. For example, they must work an overlap play, a takeover, a 1 - 2 (give and go), passing to space to move players positions on the field of play, making diagonal runs etc before they reach the target.

4. Once players are comfortable with the set-up, the coach can introduce a progression, starting with a **4 v 1 situation** attacking one way with the other three players behind their own goal. Once the team has finished their attack, these three link with the one teammate already on the field and attack one of the previous team's players (the three players not involved recover back behind their own goal, ready for their next attack).

4 v 1 (OR 5 v 2 WITH KEEPERS) ATTACKING EACH GOAL IN A PROGRESSIVE OVERLOAD SITUATION

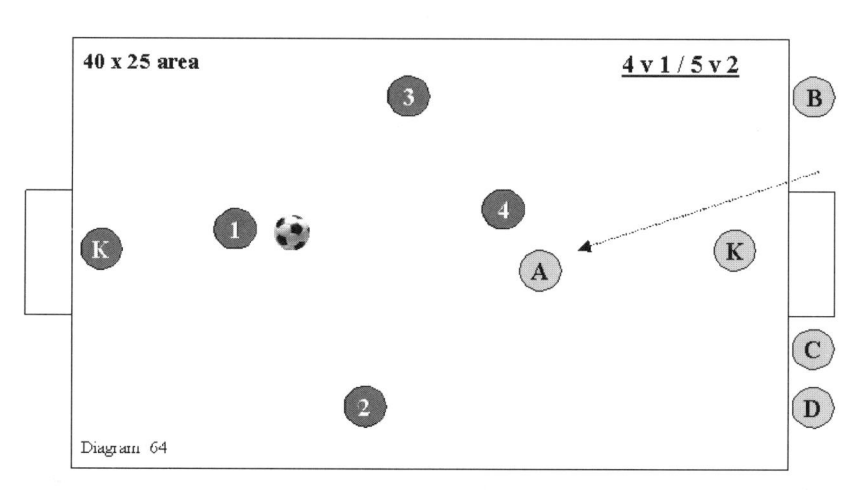

The attack by the numbers team has ended (three players leave the field, the deepest player stays on) and the letters team keeper starts the attack as this teammates break out into an attacking formation. If it is too easy, limit the players to two touches to force them to see the next pass before receiving.

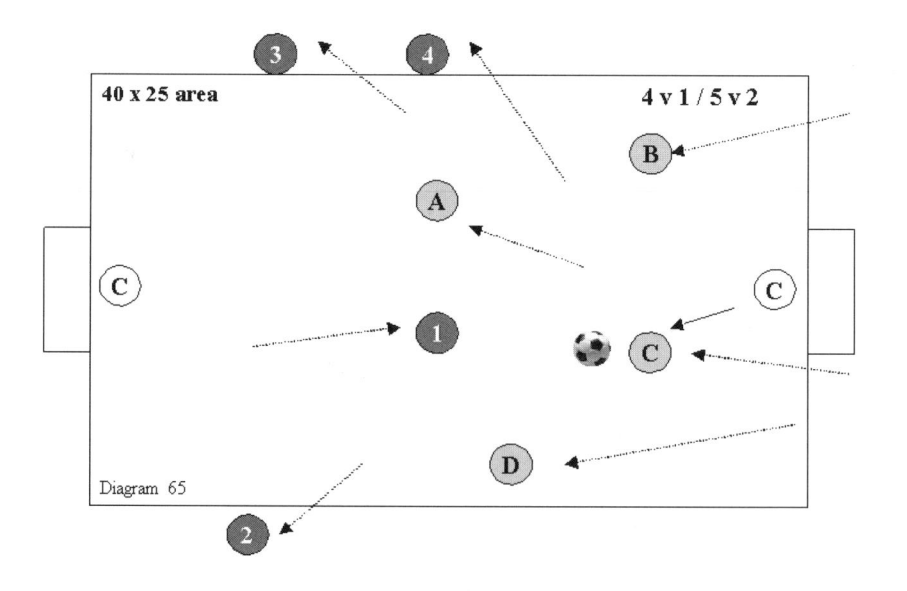

CHANGE THE SITUATION
4 v 2 (OR 5 v 3 WITH KEEPERS) OVERLOAD

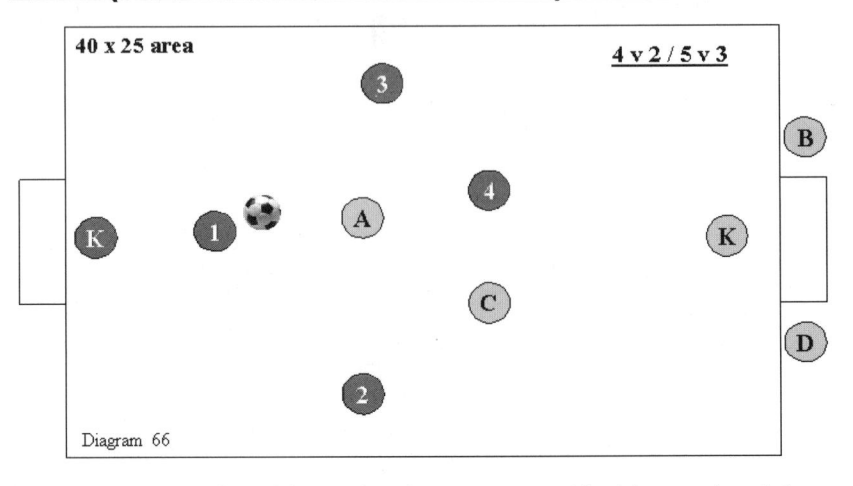

Diagram 66

1. As the players get comfortable and gain success with this overload, increase the number of defenders to make the task to attack and score more difficult (see above).

2. Ultimately build up to a 4 v 4 competitive game situation. Observe the players in their use of space, the way they support each other, how quickly they see a pass and move the ball accordingly.

3. **Progressions** - It is up to the coach to judge at what stage of development the players are. If they are well advanced in their development, still use the progressions from **4 v 0** to **4 v 1**, **4 v 2**, **4 v 3** but spend less time at each stage. The **4 v 4** situation will arrive more quickly over the course of the practice.

4. Use of progressions is very important even with very advanced players because it gives them a chance to get comfortable on the ball and to gain success from the practice initially. It is not advisable to just throw them straight into a competitive game situation and expect success from the practice.

5. It may be that players at an **early stage** of development spend most of their time in the initial practices at the 4 v 1 situation or even the 4 v 0 two team, two ball game set up. What we must focus on is making sure the players gain some success from what they practice and not move on too quickly to the next progression.

6. Developing the small sided game concept is important because on the full field of play the game consists of many S.S.G. situations with combination plays within them. What happens in the actual 8 v 8 or 11 v 11 game is a reflection on what happens in the small sided games.

ANTICIPATION, IMAGINATION, AWARENESS

4 v 4 (OR 5 v 5 WITH KEEPERS)

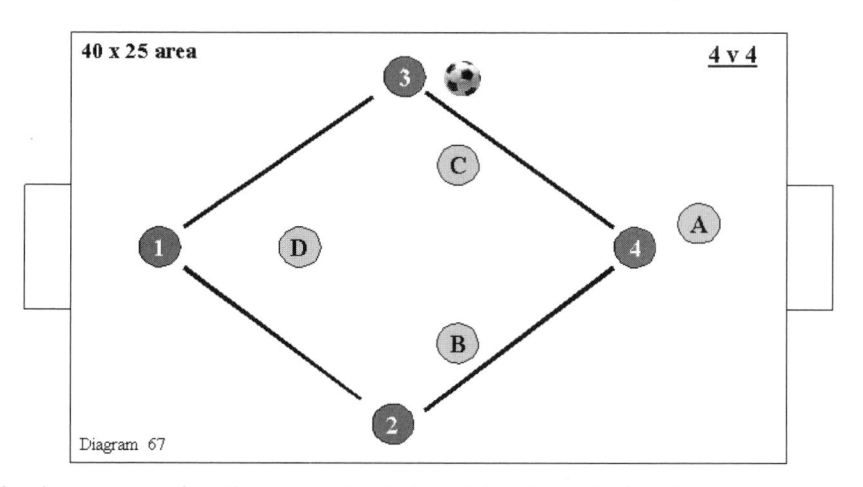

40 x 25 area

4 v 4

Diagram 67

1. This is the set up for the eventual 4 v 4 (or 5 v 5 plus keepers) competitive game situation. The coaching points below are important to use as guidelines to what you are trying to achieve in this session.

2. The attacking four should be spread out as wide and long as they can to make it difficult for the defending team to mark them. Maintenance of a rough **diamond shape** ensures good angles and distances of support wherever the ball may be.

3. The use of the A.I.A. principles is very important in the development of this game concept and you can ensure they are applied by conditioning the game. For example, make it one and two touch play.

Coaching Points

a) **Correct Positioning** when attacking and defending.
b) **Maintaining Possession** and dictating the direction of play by running with the ball, passing and dribbling.
c) Forward passing where possible but if not then positioning for back or sideways passing.
d) **Movement as a team** forward, backward, sideways left and right.
e) **Communication** - verbal and non verbal (body language).
f) **Techniques involved** - Controlling and Passing, receiving and turning, dribbling, shielding and shooting. Defending.

PASSING SUPPORT AND COMBINATION GAME PLAN
4 v 4 - BASIC DIAMOND SHAPE

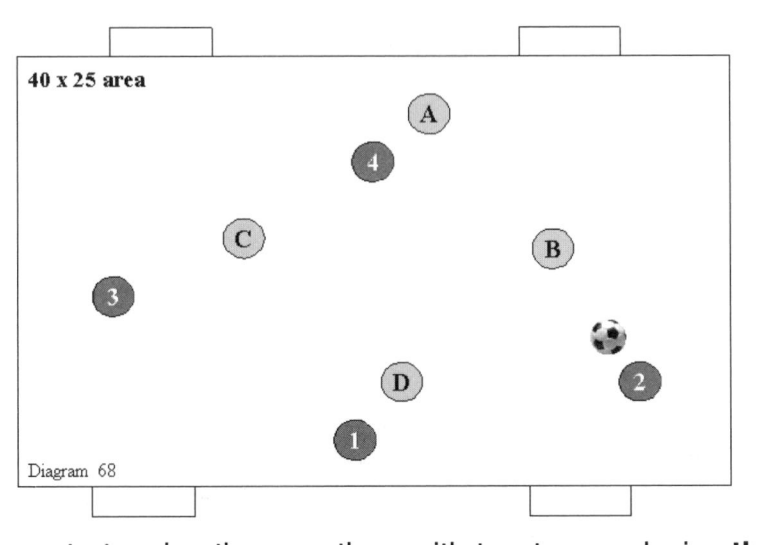

40 x 25 area

Diagram 68

1. You can start as in other practices with two teams playing **through each other** with a ball each, practicing switching play, attacking each goal in turn. Limit it to two touches to ensure quick decisions both from the player on the ball and the players off the ball who need to get in support positions early.

2. Use two wide positioned goals for each team to attack. This is designed to encourage players to spread out when they attack and **switch play**; changing direction if one route is blocked. It also encourages players on the ball to look around more as there are two areas to attack.

3. Looking for quick transition and movement off the ball to create space, but attacking the space when it is on to do so. The first thought of the player on the ball should still be "Should I dribble or pass the ball forward?".

Coaching Points

a) **Creating Space** - for yourself and your teammates.
b) **Decision** - When, Where and How to pass the ball.
c) **Technique** - The Quality of the pass (Accuracy, Weight, Angle).
d) **Support Positions** of teammates (Angle, Distance and Communication) in front and behind.
e) **Switching Play** using width in attack.

ANTICIPATION, IMAGINATION, AWARENESS

DEFENDING GAME PLAN
4 v 4 - BASIC DIAMOND SHAPE

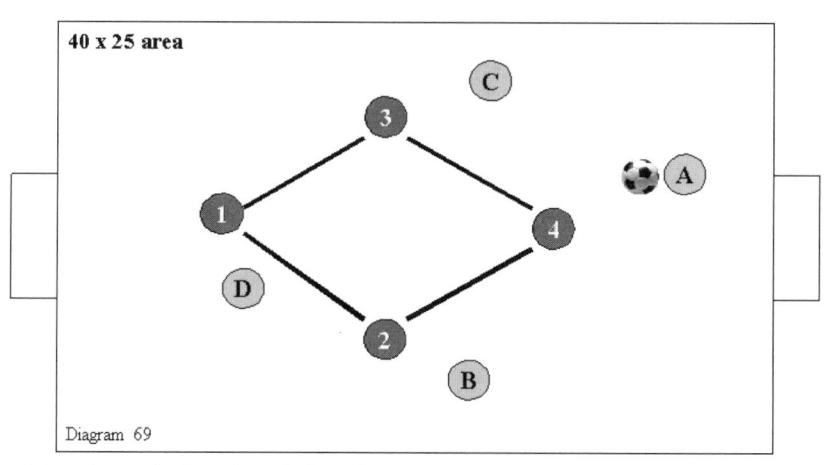

Diagram 69

1. The main idea here is for the defending team to **condense** the area the ball can be played into. The defending team becomes a diamond within the opponent's attacking diamond. (4) forces (A) one way and the rest of the team adjust their positions off this. (3) protects the space inside but can **close down** (C) if the ball is passed, (2) and (1) are the same scenario and this results in the diamond being **shorter and tighter**.

2. As the opponents move, the defending team must move to compensate. Also, if any pass is played behind (1), (2) or (3) they should be first to the ball.

Coaching Points

a) Pressure - 1 v 1 defending to win the ball, delay or force a bad pass.
b) Support - position of immediate teammate (angle, distance and communication).
c) Cover - positions of teammates beyond the supporting player.
d) Recovering and Tracking should the ball go past our position, recovery run to goal side of the ball and tracking the run of a player.
e) Double-Teaming - (A) passes to (C), (3) closes (C) down from in front, (4) follows along the path of the ball to close down from behind or slightly to the side. (4) Closes in such a way as to obstruct a bass back to (A).
f) Regaining Possession and **creating Compactness** from the back (pushing up as a unit).

3. The objectives of defending are to **disrupt** the other team's build-up, make play **predictable**, prevent forward passes and ultimately regain possession of the ball.

4. Techniques include - pressuring, marking, tackling and winning the ball.

ANTICIPATION, IMAGINATION, AWARENESS

SHOOTING GAME WITH KEEPERS

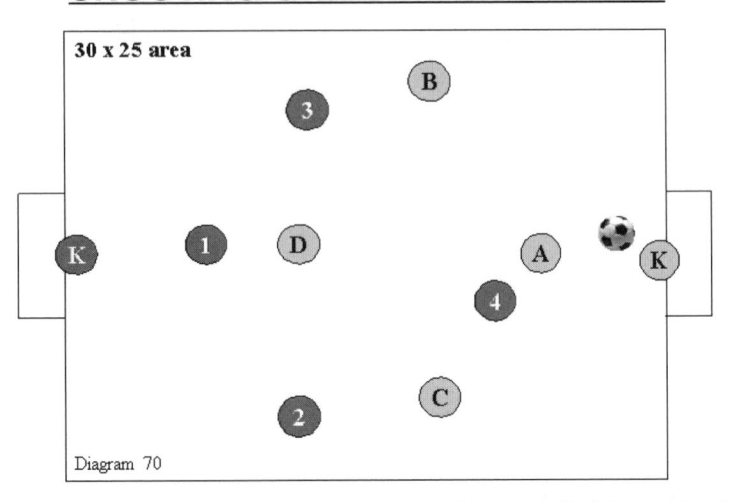

Diagram 70

1. Two large goals to encourage success. Shorter field results in lots of shots on goal because players are nearly always in shooting positions. Initially, have the two team / two ball set up so **no opposition** to enable players to work both ways to get lots of shots in. Once a team has worked a position to shoot and has done so, that team's keeper sets up another attack.

2. Progress it to the competitive even sided game.

Coaching Points

a) Quick shooting.
b) Rebounds.
c) Transitions.
d) Quick break counter attack.

3. Players must be particularly aware of where teammates are, where the opposition are and the keeper's position because the space to work in is small and the time they have on the ball is short.

4. Development of the **mental side** of the game in terms of the A.I.A. program (i.e. seeing situations quickly and acting upon them) is very important to the player to help him gain success by scoring goals. The shorter and sharper the practice, the less time the players have to make the correct decisions to be successful. This game trains players to cope with these pressure situations.

ANTICIPATION, IMAGINATION, AWARENESS

DRIBBLING GAME

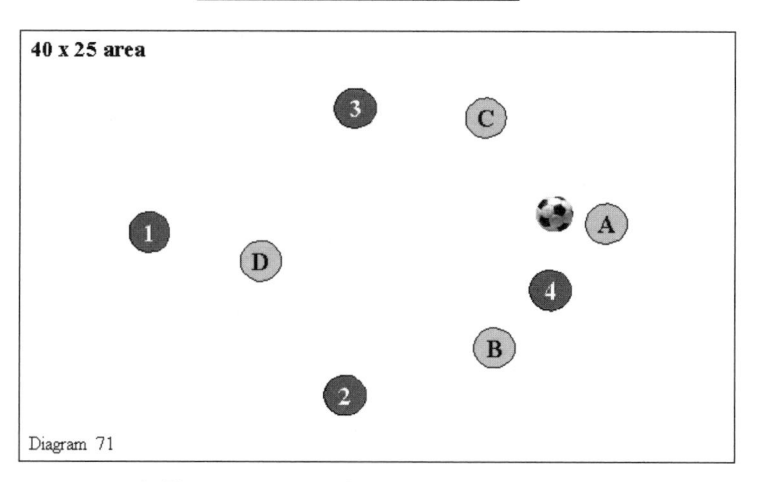

40 x 25 area

Diagram 71

1. **No goals** are used. To score, a player must dribble the ball over the goal line. Looking to encourage 1 v 1's, work on improving ball control with quick movement and decision making. This practice can be applied with the same principles with larger numbers of players such as 6 v 6 etc.

Coaching Points

a) **Creating Space** - For yourself to receive the ball.

b) **Decision** - When and where to dribble (less likely in the defending third, most likely in the attacking third).

c) **Technique** -Tight Close Control on receiving the ball, use of body to dummy an opponent, ability to change pace and direction, established dribbling skills, a positive attitude to beat the player.

d) **Runs of Teammates** - To support or to take opponents away to leave a 1 v 1 situation.

e) **End Product** - beating an opponent in a 1 v 1 situation.

While with the A.I.A. program I am encouraging players to make quick observations and quick decisions, often resulting in a player passing the ball early to avoid being caught in possession, it also helps players who are good at dribbling by enabling them to **identify situations** in advance to allow them to get in a good position to take a player on in a **1 v 1** situation. This could include opening the body up to receive and face up to an opponent, seeing the immediate opponent has no cover on so you can attack 1 v 1, seeing where the defender is early and identifying the best side to attack, seeing you have no support so have to attack 1 v 1 etc.

SMALL SIDED 6 v 6 GAMES

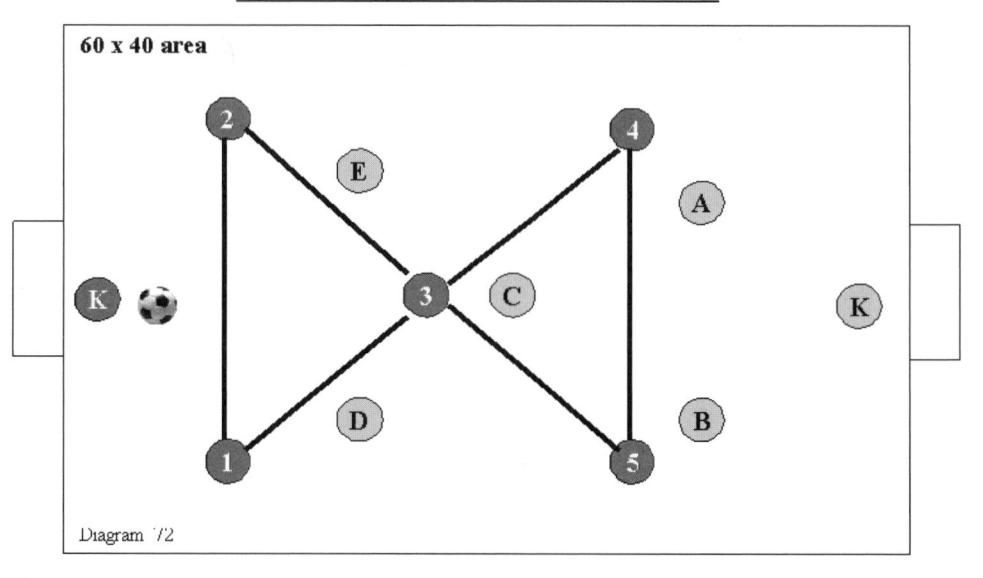

Diagram 72

1. The basic shape is a double triangle, again a positional theme where players are encouraged to interchange then return to a basic shape when the time is right. You could use a 2 - 2 - 1 formation also to allow a 2 v 1 overload at the defensive end.

2. As in the previous S.S.G's the coach needs to focus on the principles established with the A.I.A. program and get the players to apply them in the S.S.G. concept.

Coaching points

a) Create Space - players spread out to be in position to receive the ball.
b) Decision - when, where and how to pass.
c) Technique - Quality of the pass (Accuracy, weight and angle).
d) Support Positions - of teammates (angle, distance, and communication).
e) End Product - shots on goal, rebounds.
f) The **themes** you can concentrate on one at a time include, Creating Space as a team, Forward passes to Feet and Space, Switching Play as a team, Running with the Ball, One and Two Touch Play, Passing and Support Play, Diagonal Runs without the Ball (diagonal runs, Overlaps, blindside runs, under laps), Forward diagonal Runs to Receive, Receiving and Turning, When and Where to Dribble.

EXAMPLES OF PROGRESSIONS IN A SMALL SIDED GAME

A 6 v 1 GAME OVERLOAD SITUATION

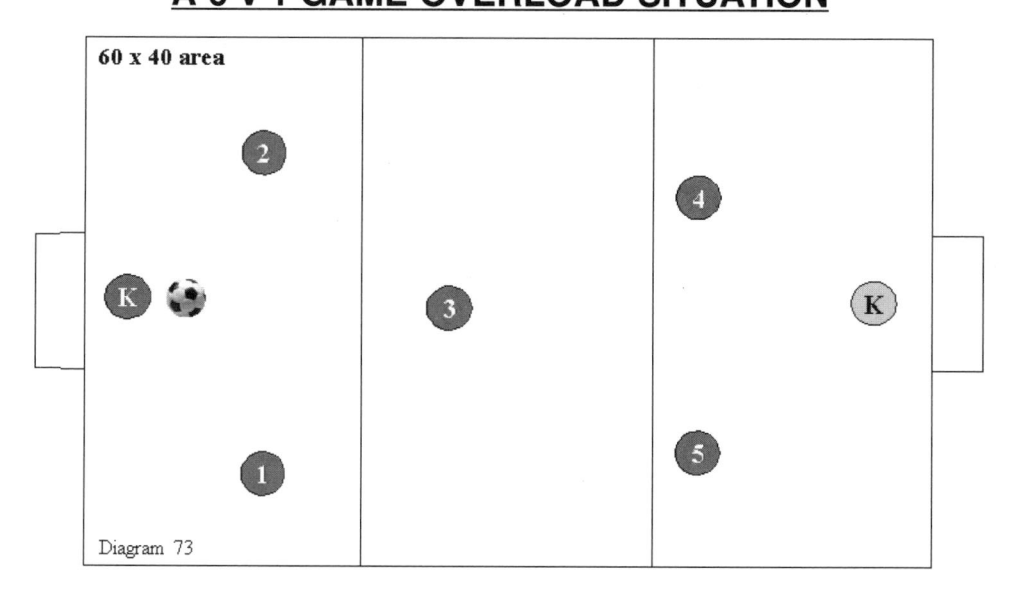

Diagram 73

A 6 v 4 GAME OVERLOAD SITUATION

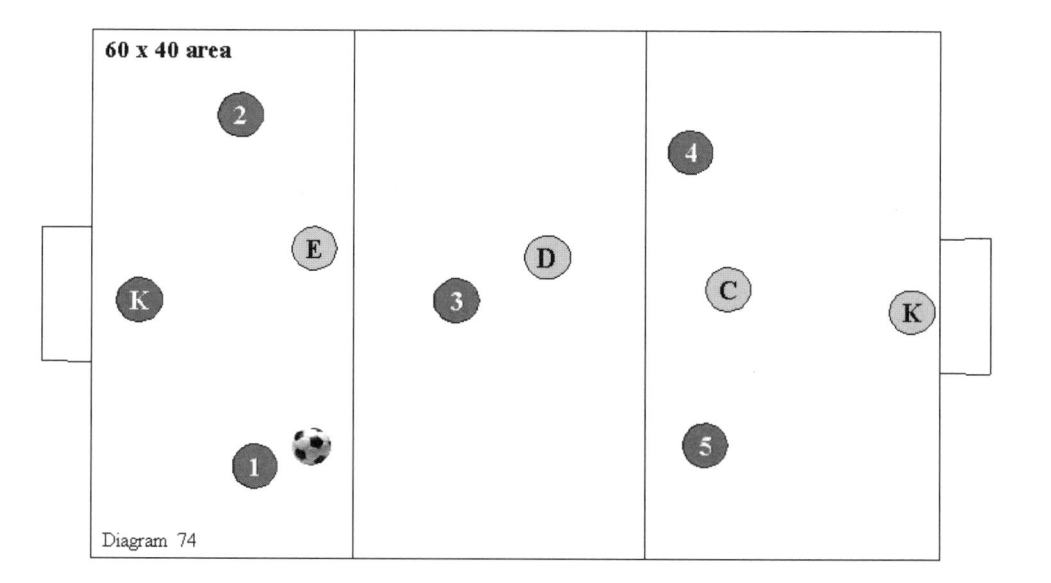

Diagram 74

A 6 v 6 TWO TEAM / TWO BALL GAME SITUATION

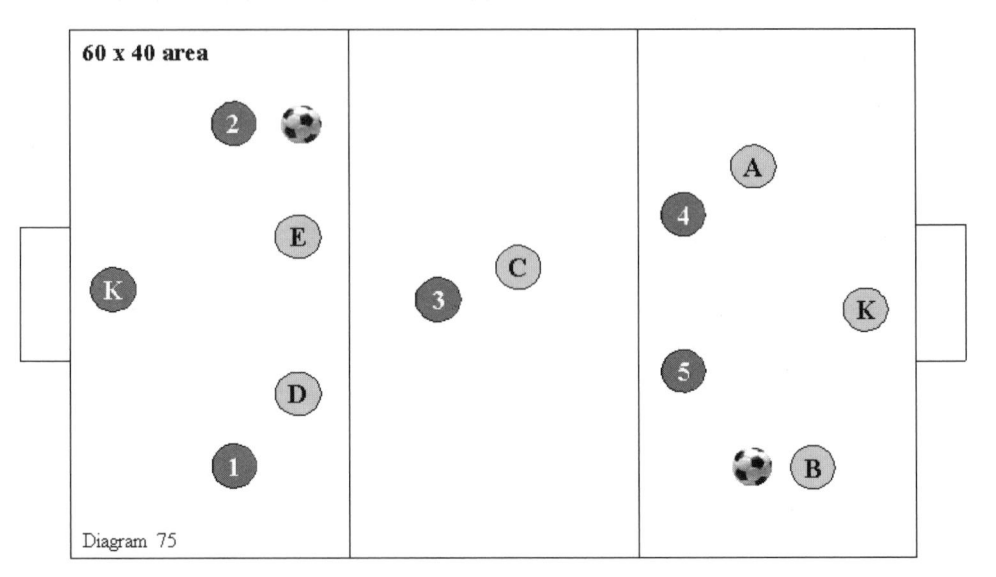

Diagram 75

1. Begin with each team playing **through** the other team, developing the particular **theme** you want to work on.

2. As soon as one move ends another begins from your goalkeeper. Players must get back into position quickly to start again.

3. Work on movement of players playing from the back through to the midfielders who receive and turn and pass to the strikers to get a shot on goal.

4. Vary it by playing from the back to the strikers directly. The strikers lay off to the supporting midfield players who then shoot on goal or make a pass for the other striker to get a shot on goal.

5. Work on passing the ball through the team and then switching the point of attack from one side to the other.

6. With no opposition, you can maintain possession and practice different types of moves without worrying about losing the ball. This helps to ensure the move can be successful from the beginning to the end. This will give the players confidence in working as a team.

RUNNING WITH THE BALL IN A SMALL SIDED 6 v 6 GAME

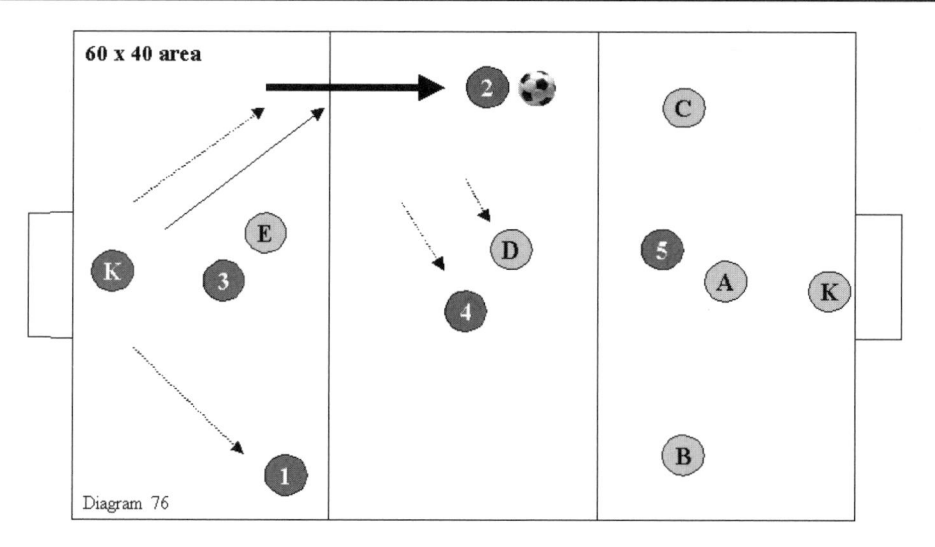

Diagram 76

1. Here the theme is **running with the ball,** particularly from the back. Use the progressions to get it going.

Coaching Points

a) Creating Space - Players break wide to receive the ball from the keeper.
b) Decision - Can I run with the ball or do I pass?
c) Technique - Key factors of running with the ball: head up, good first touch, run in a straight line (the shortest route forward) with pace, use the front foot to control the ball.
d) Quality of Pass / Cross / Shot / Dribble at the end of the run.
e) Support Positions - support in front, fill in behind.

When you get to 6 v 6 it may be useful to **change the shape** of the teams to 3 - 1 - 1 from a 2 - 1 - 2 so there is a **3 v 1 overload** at the back to help players run out with the ball. The space is usually in the **wide areas** for this movement. This allows for a greater chance of success in the practice until players are comfortable and confident performing the theme.

SWITCHING PLAY IN A SMALL SIDED GAME OF 6 v 6

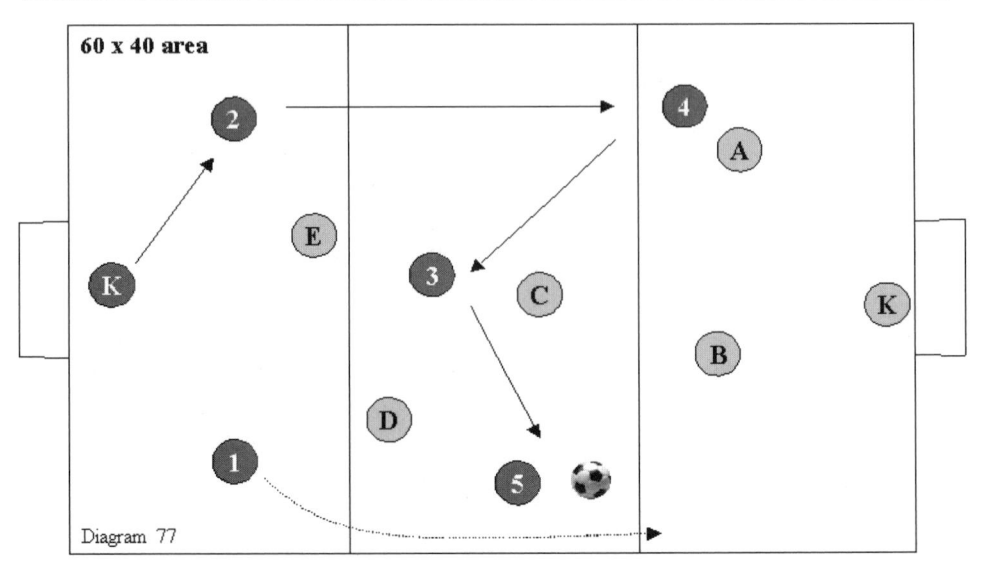

Diagram 77

1. As in **ALL** these 6 v 6 presentations, the coach should use a **progression method** to build up to the competitive 6 v 6 game situation.

2. This can begin with a **Shadow Play 6 v 0** (or just the opposing keeper) game to allow the players to get comfortable with their movements. Use the 2 - 1 - 2 system of play. The coach must decide how much of an overload is needed to build up to a 6 v 6 competitive game situation (6 v 2 , 6 v 3 etc).

3. Use the 6 v 6 game with the two-team concept before going into a competitive 6 v 6.

Coaching Points

a) **Creating Space** as individuals and a team.
b) **Decision** - When, where and how to pass the ball.
c) **Technique** - Quality of the pass, can I pass it forward or do I switch the play?
d) **Support Positions** - To switch the play (open stance to receive and pass).
e) **Switching the Play** - From one side of the field to the other.

4. In the above example the team has attacked down one side of the field but been stopped from further progress by good defending so they have switched the play to the other side. A great run by (1) on the overlap complements this move making a 2 v 1 situation on the opposite side of the field.

ANTICIPATION, IMAGINATION, AWARENESS

CREATING SPACE IN A SMALL SIDED GAME OF 6 v 6

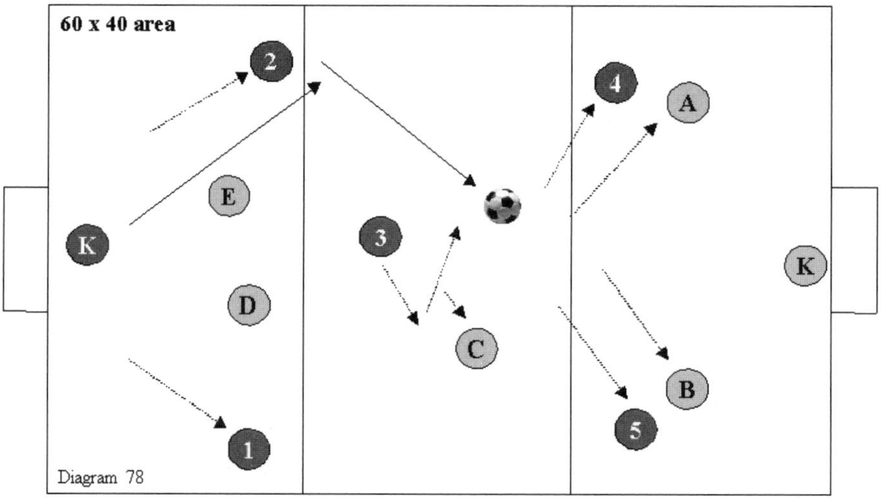

Diagram 78

1. Here the players work to get free of their markers by their **movement off the ball**. They create space for themselves and / or for their team-mates.

Coaching Points

a) Creating Space - Spreading out as a team.
b) Decision - When, where and how to Create Space.
c) Technique - of passing and receiving.
d) Support Positions of players; angles and distances, movement off the ball.

2. In the above example, (1) and (2) break wide to create space and offer two options to receive a pass from the keeper, (2) receives the pass and (3) runs off (C) to check back to receive the pass in space. (4) and (5) create space in front of the receiving player by making split runs to move (A) and (B) away from where (3) wants to attack and shoot at goal.

3. If either (A) or (B) do not track the two strikers and stay in the space in front to defend against (3), (3) can pass to whichever player got free by not being tracked on their run.

WHEN AND WHERE TO DRIBBLE
IN A SMALL SIDED 6 v 6 GAME

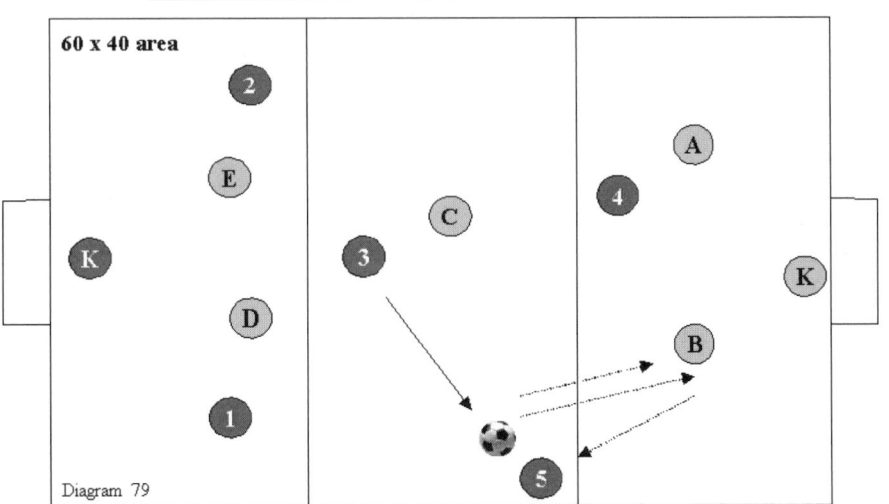

Diagram 79

1. Looking to create **1 v 1 situations** in the middle and especially the attacking thirds of the field, focusing on players with a good dribbling technique.

Coaching Points

a) Creating Space - Run the player off to check back and receive to feet. Body position half turned with the back to the touchline. Where the defender marks determines whether the attacker goes inside or outside.

b) Attitude to Dribble - Aggressive / Positive.

c) Decision - Does the attacker run, pass, cross, shoot or dribble?

d) Technique of Dribbling - when it is on to dribble. How to dribble using moves.

e) Safety and Risk Areas of the Field - where it is on to dribble.

f) Runs of the players - to support or create space.

2. Here (5) runs off (B) to create space behind to come back and receive the ball to feet. (5) must shape up with his back to the touchline to be able to see the entire field and options available. If (B) doesn't follow, (5) can get the pass in front to attack the goal, using (4) to create a 2 v 1 position.

RECEIVING AND TURNING
IN A SMALL SIDED 6 v 6 GAME

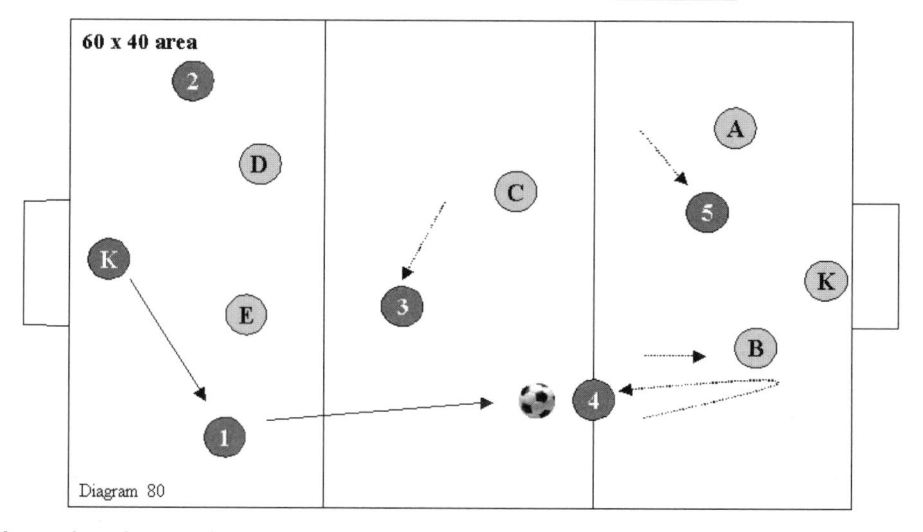

Diagram 80

1. Here the theme is **receiving and turning,** particularly in the middle and attacking thirds.

Coaching Points

a) **Creating Space** by movement off the defenders.
b) **Decision** - When and where to receive and turn.
c) **Technique** - How to receive and turn. The best way, if there is time, is to run the marker off and return to the space created for by that movement.
d) **Quality of the Pass** into the receiver for ease of control.
e) **Positions of Support** of teammates in front and behind the player on the ball.

2. In the above example (4) runs the defender (B) off away from the ball to check back to receive the pass. (3) positions to support behind as can (1) also but if (4) has turned, (5) makes a run into a receiving position of support in front of the ball to take a shot or create a 2 v 1 situation with (4) by losing the marking of (A). If (4) is a very good dribbler, (5) can run off (A) away from the space in front of goal to leave (4) in a 1 v 1 situation.

DIAGONAL RUNS WITHOUT THE BALL IN A 6 v 6 GAME

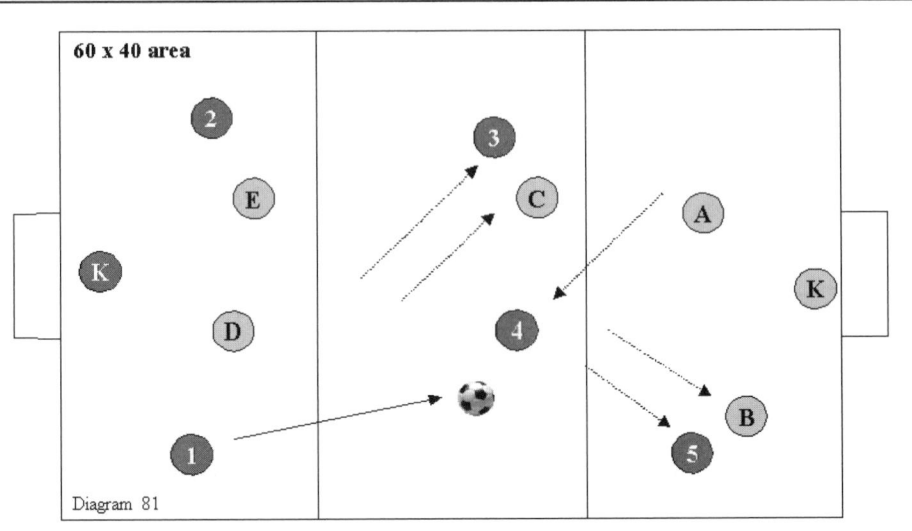

Diagram 81

1. The theme is **making diagonal runs** with or without the ball to receive or create space for a teammate. When it is a forward diagonal run, the player making it must avoid running offside in a game situation.

Coaching Points

a) Creating Space.
b) Decision -When and where to pass into the receiver.
c) Technique - Quality of pass particularly the weight, accuracy and timing.
d) Angle and Timing of the Diagonal Runs both to create space and to receive the ball.
e) Support Positions of the players.

2. In the above example (1) is on the ball to pass it forward. (5) makes a diagonal run away from the center, taking the man-marking (B) with him.(3) also makes a diagonally opposite run away from the central area taking (C) away also. This leaves space for (4) to come short with another diagonal run to receive the pass. As in receiving and turning, (4) may have run (A) off to check back if time was available to do so, thus creating more time and space on the ball.

3. Another way to create space for (4) coming short to receive would be for (5) to make a run towards (4) and cut across the path of (4)'s marker (A) to hold up his run.

FORWARD DIAGONAL RUNS TO RECEIVE
IN A 6 v 6 GAME

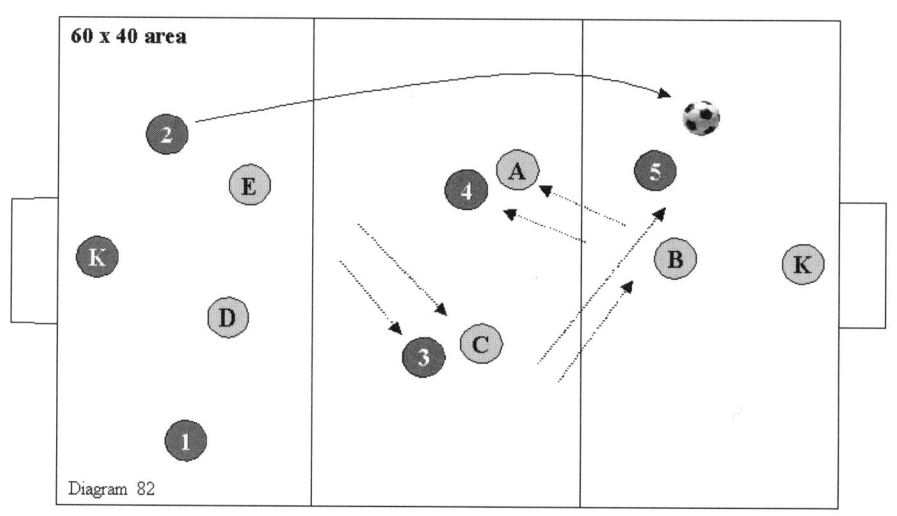

Here (4) goes short taking (A) with him. This creates space behind (A) for (5) to run into to receive the pass. (3) again runs off (C) to help clear the space.

Below, the strikers make opposite diagonal runs to get midfielder (3) in centrally.

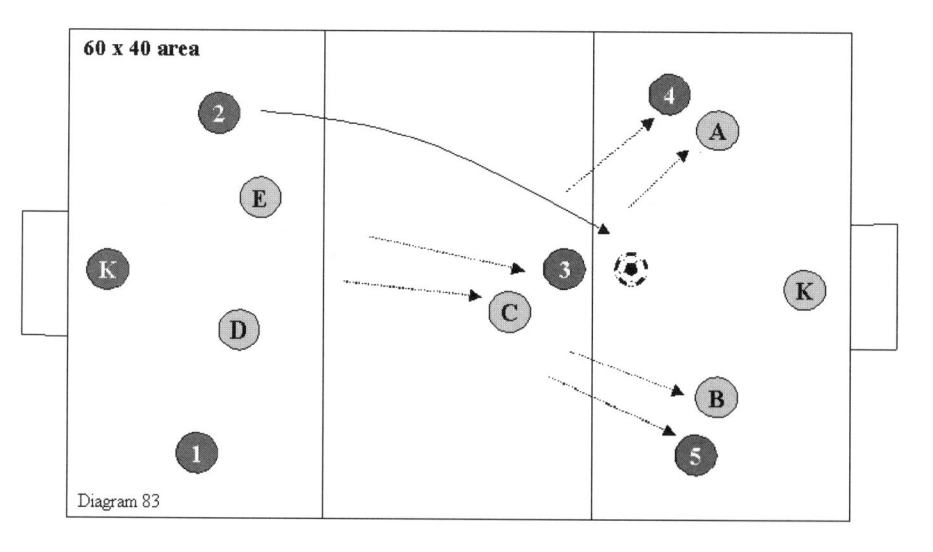

6 v 6 SESSION USING DEFENSIVE, MIDFIELD AND ATTACKING ZONES (3-2-1 or 3-1-2)

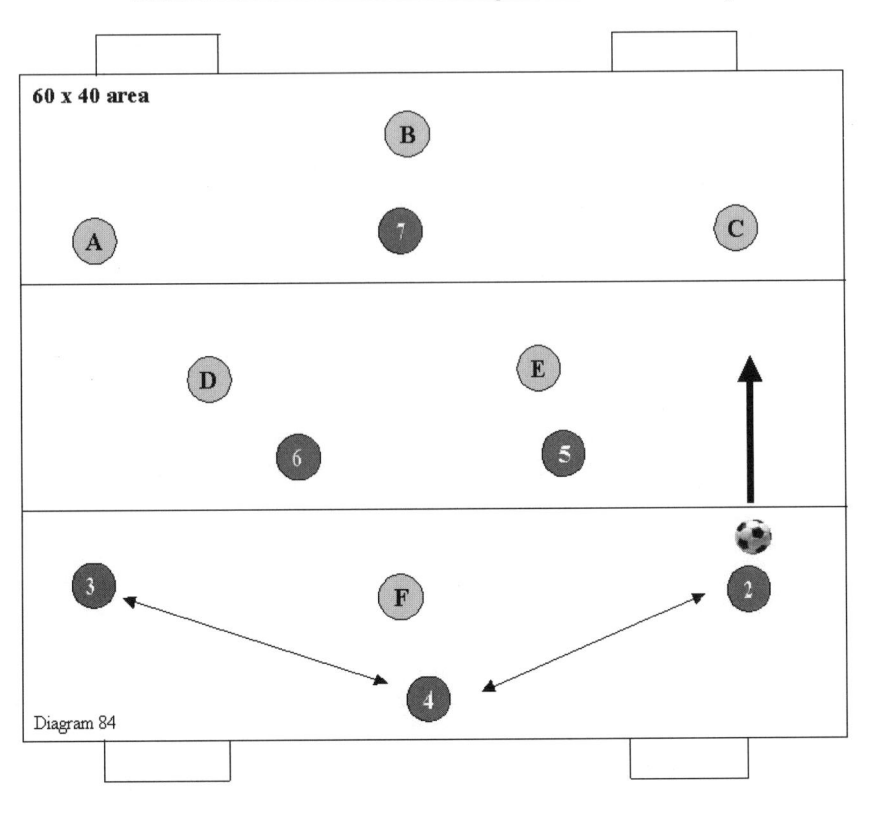

Diagram 84

1. 3 v 1 in defending third, working the ball into midfield then into attacking third. Initially, players stay in own third to learn the idea of shape through the team.

2. Ensure that link up play develops both forward and coming back. Players should get in position to support teammates early.

3. Players are allowed to move between zones and link up. As previously, once they lose possession, they drop back into own third to allow the other team to develop their play.

8 v 8 SESSION WITH COMPOSURE ZONES TO AID DEVELOPMENT

3 - 2 - 2 system

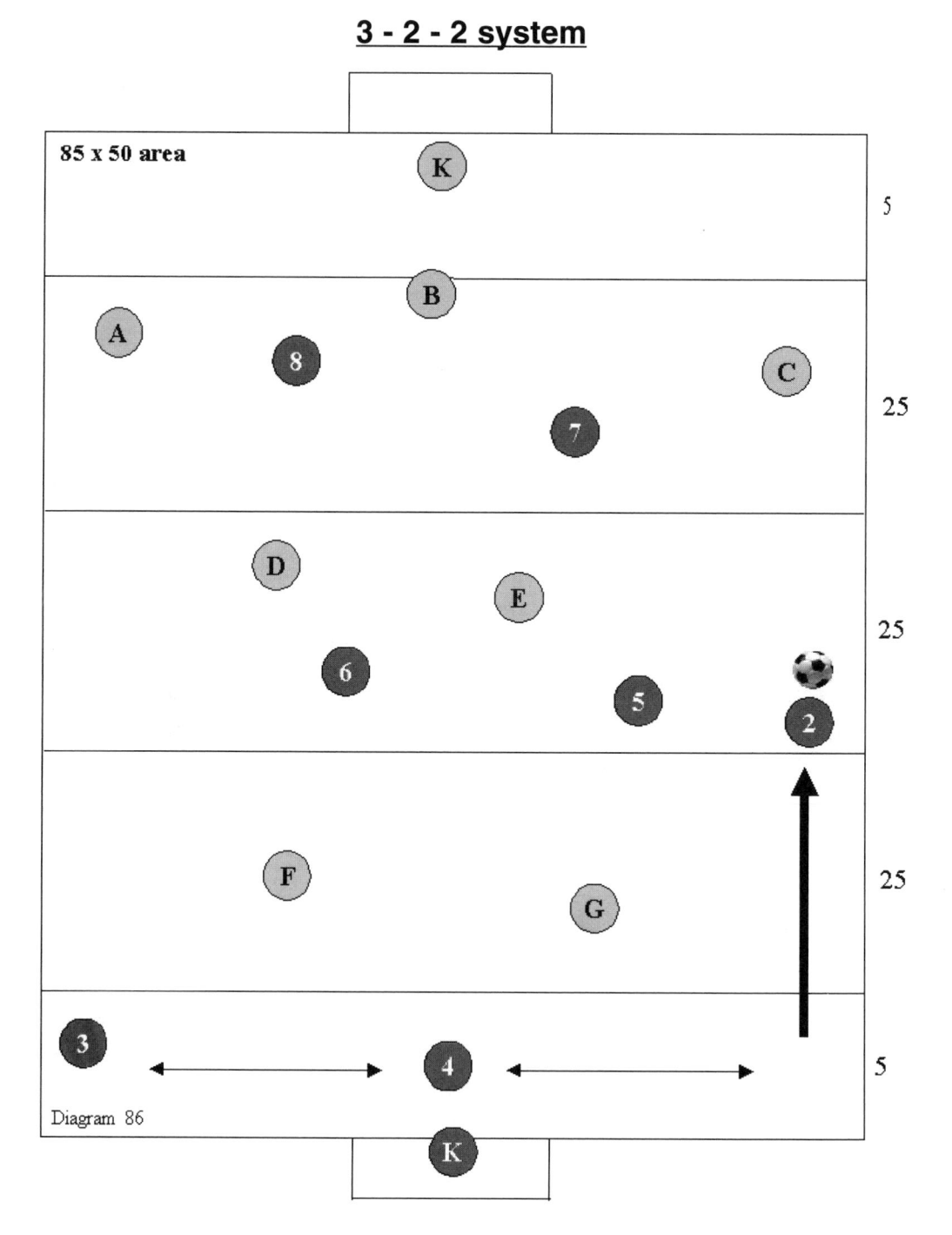

Diagram 86

1. **Overload at the back**. Two forwards can't encroach into the 5-yard composure zone. Defenders pass the ball across under no pressure until one is free to run it out, at which point attackers can now try to win it back.

2. Players stay in own zone to keep their shape. Support in front and behind.

3. **Open it up** so players can move between zones.

4. Defenders can take the ball back into the composure zone for safety. This encourages spreading out and playing from the back. Be patient, keep possession; go forward at the correct moment.

5. **Defenders** - spreading out, running with the ball, passing the ball, supporting the keeper, keeping possession, decision making.

   Midfield - receiving and turning, switching play, linking play, making runs, keeping possession, creating space, decision making.

   Forwards - as above, also supporting short and long, making diagonal runs in front of the ball, holding the ball up, lay offs, dribbles \ shots, quick decision making.

6. As ball advances, players at the back **move up**. Keep checking positions and shape of the team.

7. To get full game started, have one team standing still and let the other team play through them to get a feel for how to build up the play.

8. **Develop** this by having both teams with a ball each playing through each other where they are not under the pressure of losing the ball.

NB - If you have problems making this session work with equal numbers, build it up to the full team situation and organize 8 v 5 with only one forward, one midfielder, two defenders and a keeper in the other team.

ANTICIPATION, IMAGINATION, AWARENESS

Development - 3-2-2 System

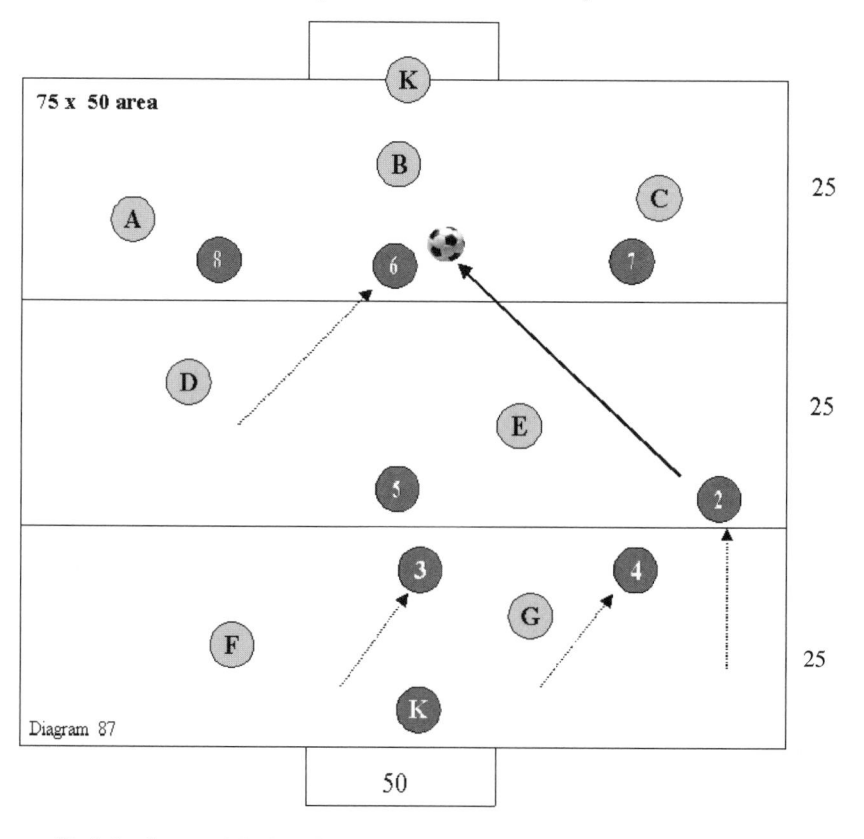

Diagram 87

1. Play **offside** from thirds. Players **interchange** between zones one at a time, always returning to original set-up. Check the balance of the team with and without the ball. Create a 3 v 2 in midfield zone with player (2) moving up. (2) could play the ball into the attacking third and player (6) could join in to make a 3 v 3.

2. Player (2) fills his place in midfield. If he loses possession, players either drop back in or you can develop the session to include pressing to regain the ball. (e.g. If you are losing the game, go **full high pressure** and leave three players in attacking third, two in midfield third and two in defensive third).

3. **Condition** - Can only score if all players are over the defensive third line. This reinforces staying compact vertically.

4. **Restrict number of touches** on the ball if the players are able to do so to encourage **quick passing** and movement and to improve the speed of decision making.

5. **Vary play** by encouraging defenders to pass **directly** to the forwards. Midfield players can then support them facing the opponents goal (easier to support rather than receiving and having to turn with the ball).

6. If you have problems making the session work with equal numbers, reduce the game to an **8 v 5** situation using one forward, one midfield er, two defenders and a keeper on the opponent's team until the players are comfortable, then go into the full workout.

POSITIONAL DEVELOPMENT

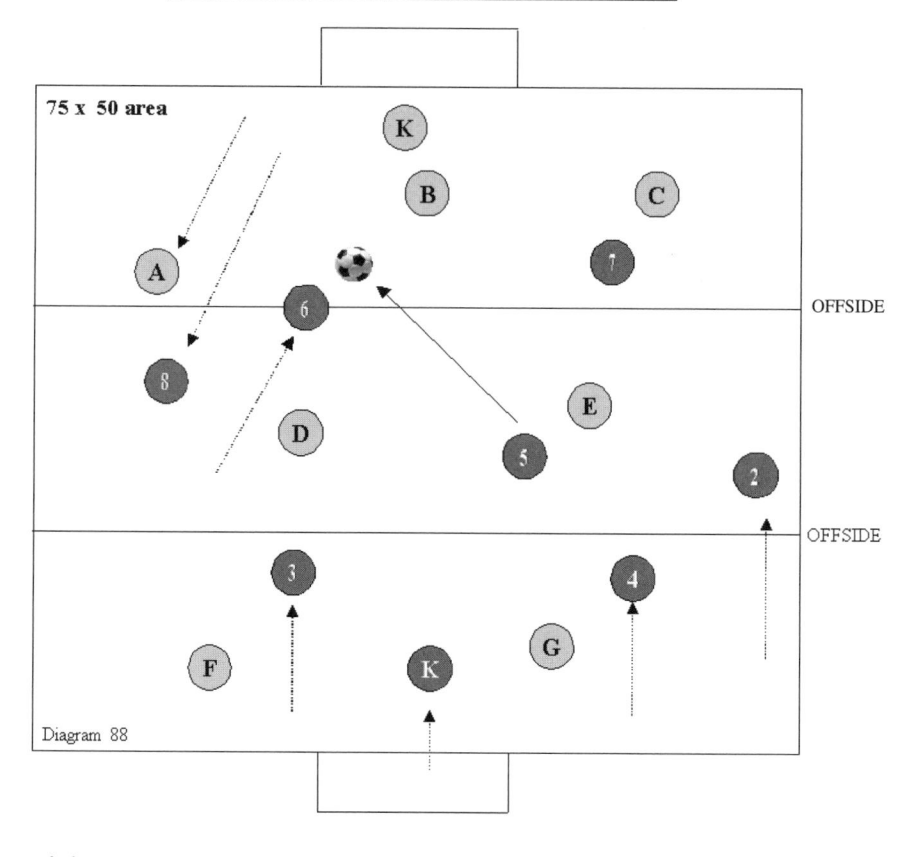

Diagram 88

1. Player (5) is on the ball. (8) comes short to receive and his defender tracks him, creating space in behind. Player (6) changes position with (8) with a diagonal run to receive the pass.

2. If defender marking (8) stays (doesn't track 8), the pass should be to (8)'s feet so he can turn and attack 1 v 1, or (5) can overlap and create a 2 v 1 wide.

3. In possession, (3) and (4) push out to leave opponents offside.

4. **Transition** - if possession is lost and for example (6) and (5) finish in front of (8) and (7) up the field, (8) and (7) can fill in for them and defend midfield.

POSSIBLE PASSING OPTIONS

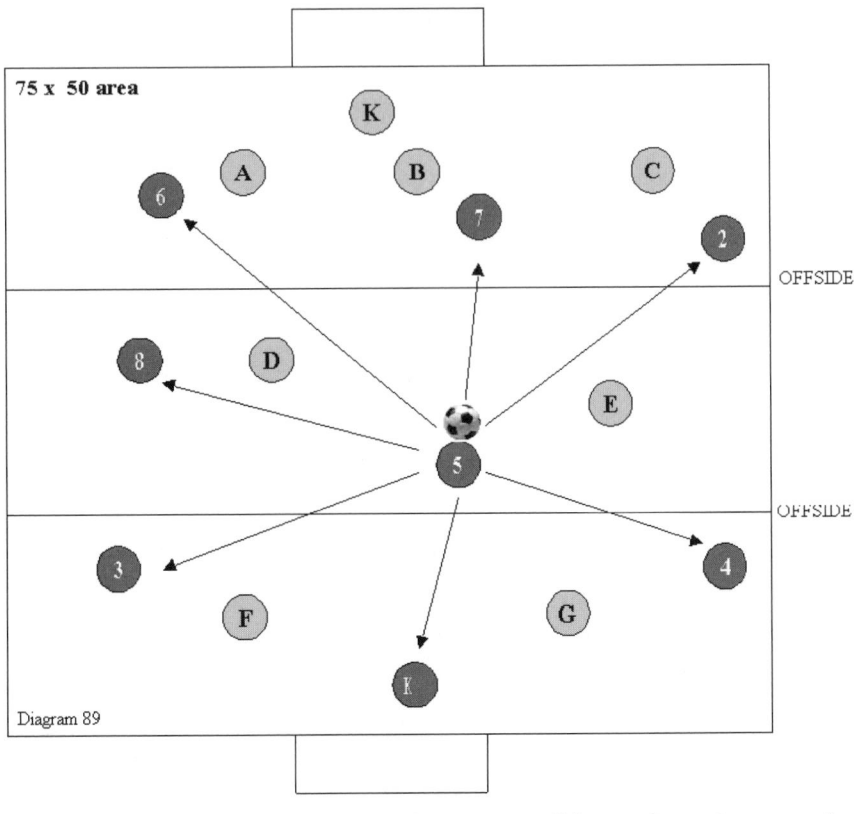

Diagram 89

5. Player (5) on the ball. He has three possible options to pass forward (e.g. to (6) , (7) or (2) who continues the run). If he can't go forward because of pressure, he can go to the side to (8) or back to (3), (4) and the keeper to keep possession until the situation allows for a forward pass again (you won't obviously get all these options to pass but it shows how it can work).

6. Caution - in attack, be aware of quick counter if opponents win the ball i.e. we have 2 v 2 at the back.

Discussion - You can get so much work into this session. Every time you look there may be a new situation to effect. Choose a theme and stick with it and when you have established it with the players, only then move onto another theme (you can again use the same set-up, as it is so flexible).

TRAINING SESSION TO PRACTICE TEAM SHAPE

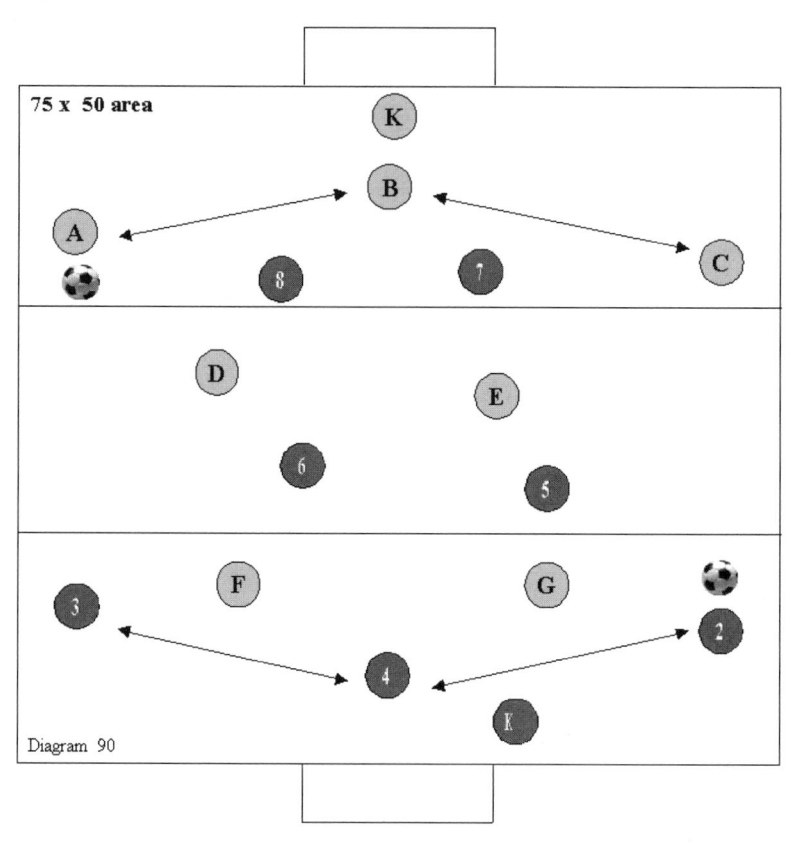

Diagram 90

1. Two balls, a ball each team, shadow play but with opposition to play through. Each team takes up their positions on the field depending on the position of their own ball.

2. Effectively, there are two separate games going on. Initially have the players stay in their thirds to establish a team shape, progress to one player only crossing over a zone, then open it up. Finish with a game using two balls.

ANTICIPATION, IMAGINATION, AWARENESS

TRANSITION GAMES
MAINTAINING SHAPE AND BALANCE

The following set-ups can be used with different numbers of players to suit training needs (odd number use a free player). You will achieve the same results, be it 4 v 4, 6 v 6, 7 v 7, 8 v 8, 9 v 9 up to 11 v 11.

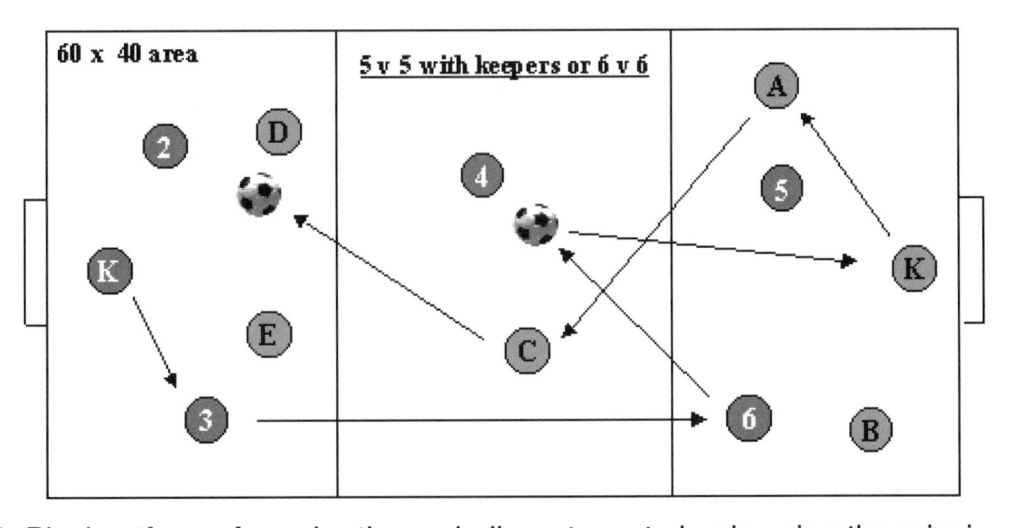

60 x 40 area

5 v 5 with keepers or 6 v 6

1. Playing **through** each other, a ball per team to begin using the principles developed with the use of the A.I.A. program. Players stay in own zones to begin, maintaining shape throughout the team. They can shoot at the end of the move then start a new move from the keeper. The coach can suggest options using one word to get them to think about different types of movement: **forward**, **back**, **switch**, etc, then let the players work it out themselves.

2. Develop by allowing players to cross over zones to support each other. Still no opposition, just two teams playing through each other. Once the move is over the team returns to their original team shape. Initially, have the same players drop back to their respective zones.

3. **Develop** - Have players return to the original team shape but encourage other players to do it, depending on where they are on the field. An example; (2) runs forward and finishes in the attacking third (an attacking overlap run in a game), wait to see if the players recognize that (4) drops back into the defensive third to cover and (2) drops back to the middle third (shortest route back), so (2) only has to get back 15 yards instead of 30 yards.

4. **Develop** - Into a **competitive game** situation. Defending players must stay in their own zones to allow the attacking concept to take shape.

ANTICIPATION, IMAGINATION, AWARENESS

PLAYERS STAYING IN THEIR OWN THIRDS

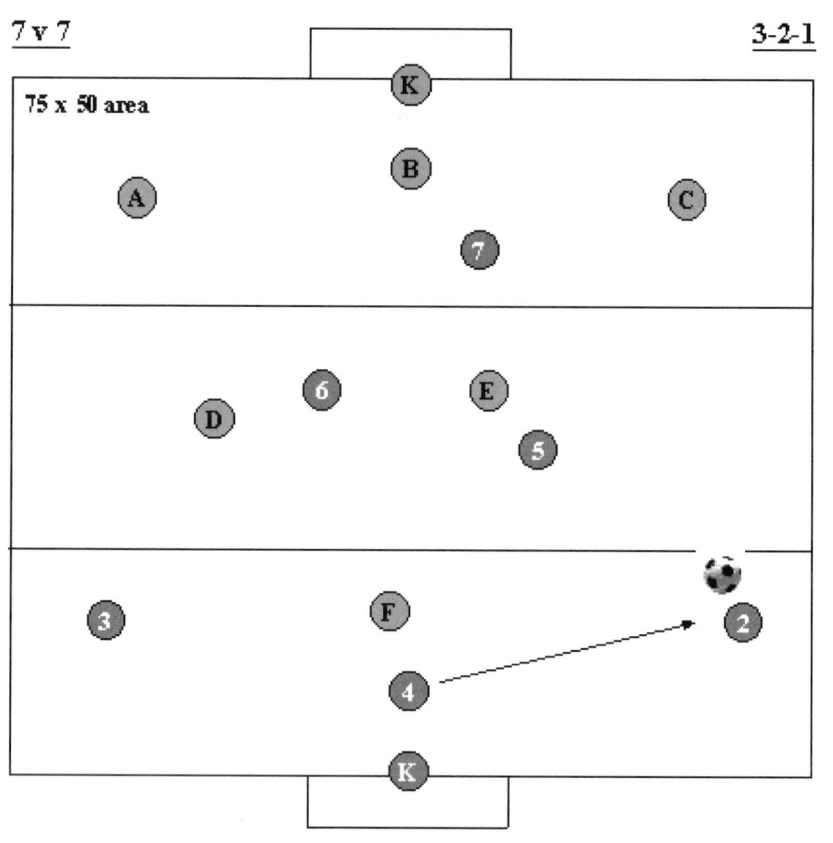

1. To ensure the players have a chance to build up the play from the back, have a 3 v 1 overload at each defensive third to begin the session.

2. We are looking to be successful with offensive play building up from the back and this gives it a greater chance of success. This creates a positive reinforcement for the players.

3. As they get better at this and gain success you can change it to a 3 v 2 situation so it is more difficult to achieve.

ANTICIPATION, IMAGINATION, AWARENESS

TRANSITIONS BETWEEN THIRDS

8 v 8   3-2-2

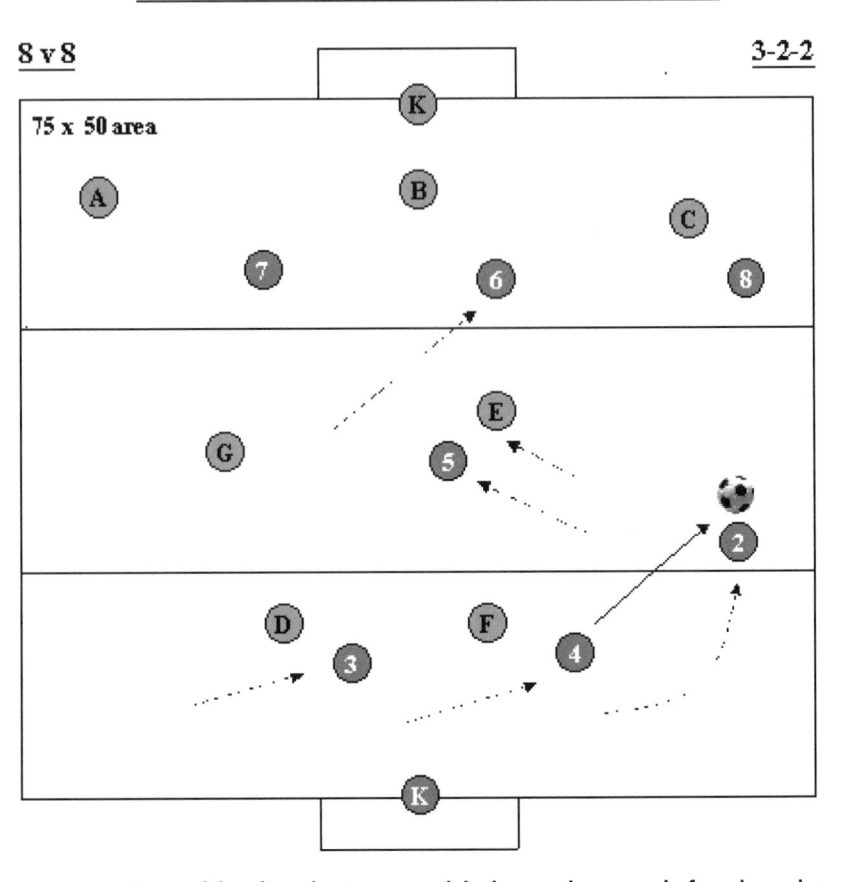

75 x 50 area

1. Now we are transitioning between thirds and as a defender changes the balance in midfield from a 2 v 2 into a 3 v 2, a midfielder then moves into the attacking third to change the balance from a 2 v 3 into a 3 v 3.
2. (5) Clears the space for (2) to bring the ball forward. (4) and (3) cover across behind the field to support and be in a good position to cover should the move break down. This is clearing the space in front of the ball and filling in behind the ball.
3. (6) makes a run into the attacking third to be another target for (2) to pass to.
4. If the player can't go forward and has to play it back, ensure that the players behind the ball get in positions where they are free to receive it and able to support the player on the ball.

ANTICIPATION, IMAGINATION, AWARENESS

TRANSITIONS OVER THIRDS

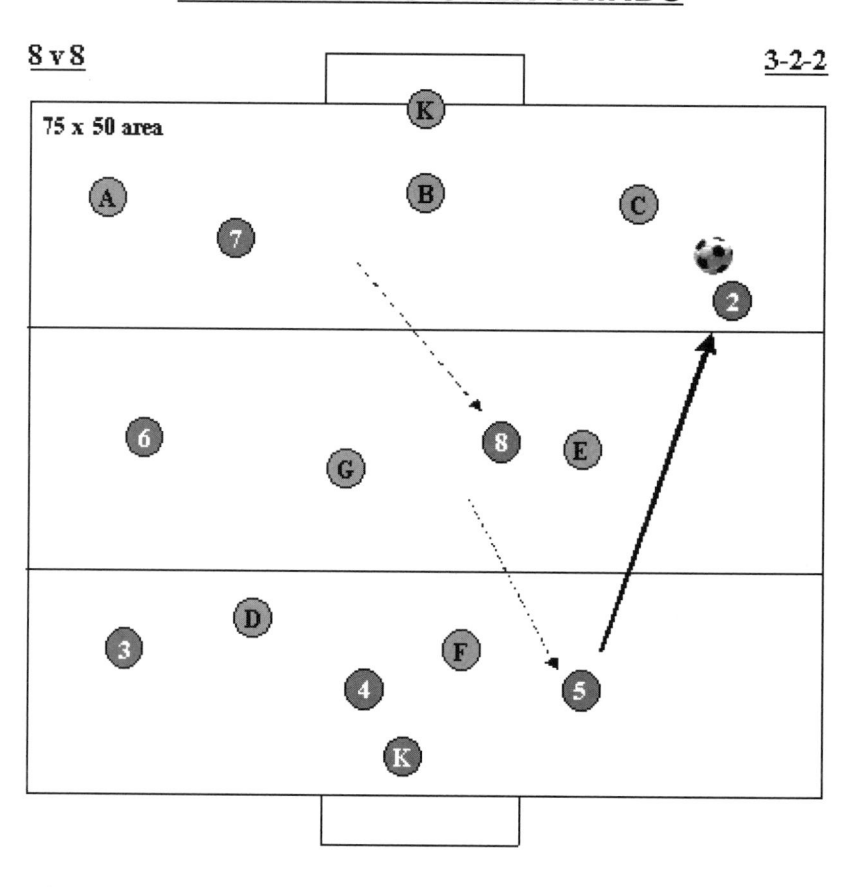

1. (2) on the ball may run over three zones with the ball. If and/or when the move breaks down and the opposition win the ball, (5) can replace (2) and (8) can replace (5) so each player gets back the team shape by the shortest route. This encourages particularly the fullbacks to attack down the flanks, as they know they don't face a 50-yard run back in a game situation because a teammate will cover for them. It may only result in a 10 or 15 yard run, saving energy and time.

2. This method of playing gives **FREEDOM** to the players. You can encourage the players to communicate with each other as this is happening. For example, (2) runs forward with the ball and instructs (5) to be prepared to cover.

3. Players change back to their positions as soon as they can within the game.

4. Players can run the ball in, pass it in, or pass it in to a runner from their own zone.

ANTICIPATION, IMAGINATION, AWARENESS

OVERLAP PLAY

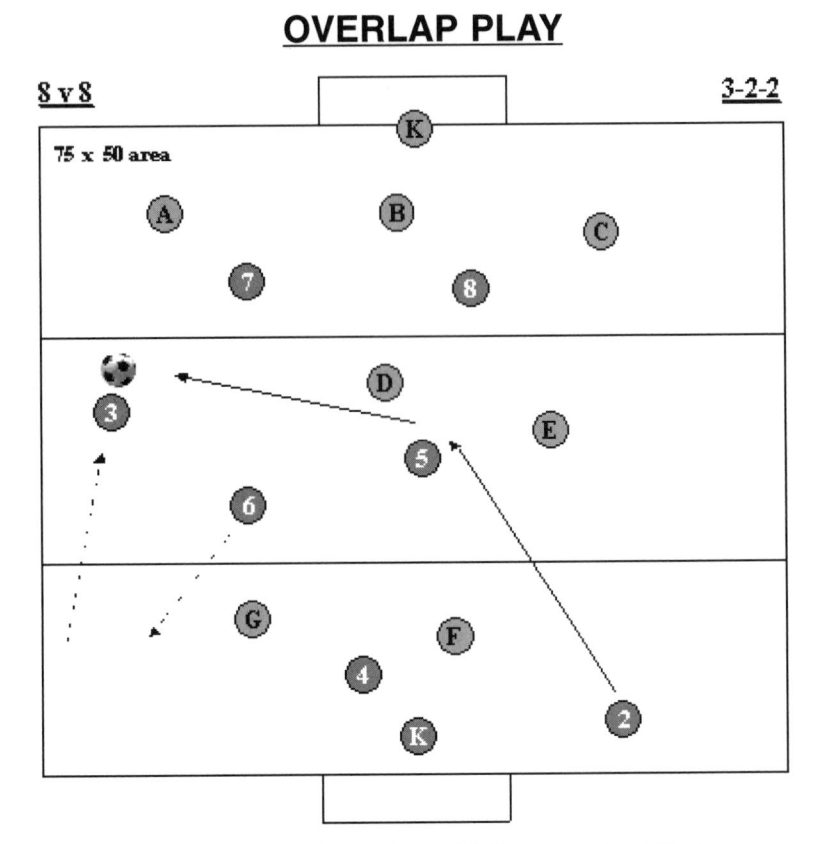

1. Player (2) passes the ball into the middle zone to (5), (3) moves up from the defensive zone to the middle zone to support. This type of **transition movement** is important because it allows players to move freely between the zones knowing they will have a teammate covering for them.

2. **Develop** - Have offside from the defensive third of the field, encouraging pressing up.

3. In terms of the opposition this rapid movement and transition makes it difficult for defenders to pick players up, to read what the attacking team is doing and how it is playing. Usually (D) would be marking (6) but now has to think about marking (3).

4. This means defenders aren't just defenders, midfielders aren't just midfielders and attackers aren't just attackers. They work to help each other through the three units of the team and are free to mix the game up. This is **total soccer,** played to encourage the free movement of players throughout the teams.

OVERLOAD IN ATTACK TO MAINTAIN POSSESSION

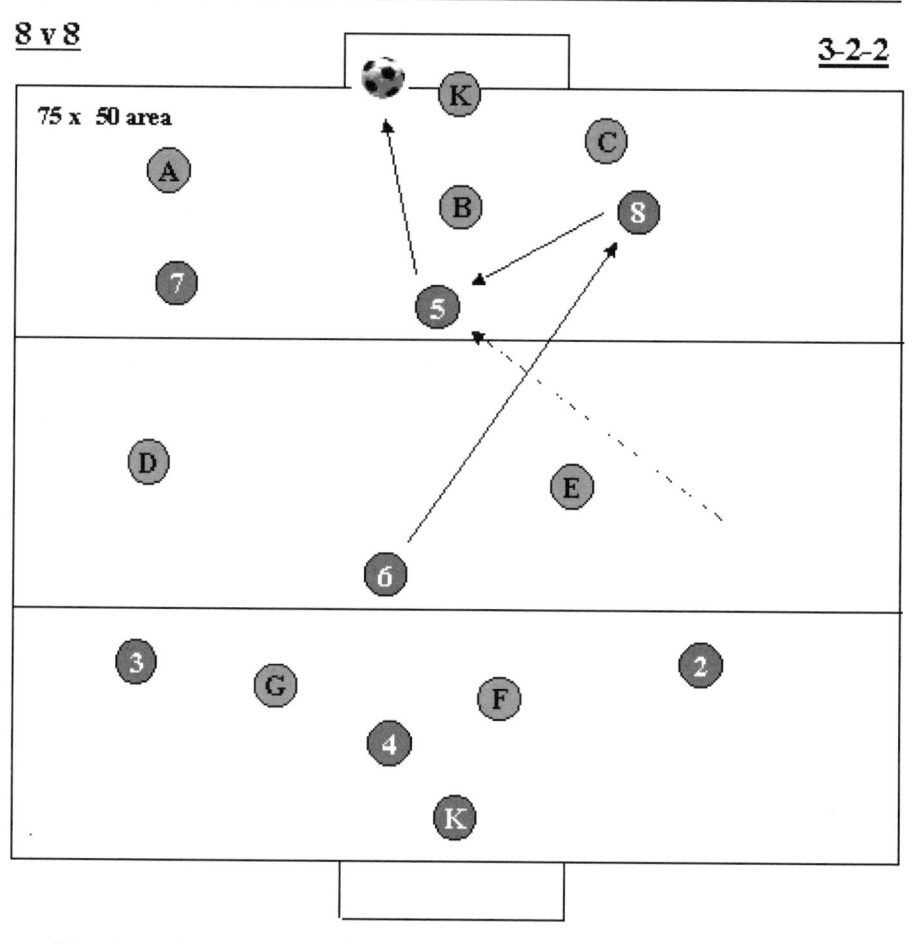

1. Here (6) plays the ball to (8) and (5) makes a run off the ball to support in the attacking third. (8) may be able to lay the ball off for (5) to shoot at goal.

2. You can practice this session with different numbers of players to get the same effect, building up to an 11 v 11 game.

3. Transitions can depend on the stage of the game; if your team is a goal down then (7) would probably stay in the attacking third instead of covering for (5) to keep an **overload situation** there, but the basis of the session is to show how to maintain a **balanced shape** in your team.

SWITCHING POSITIONS

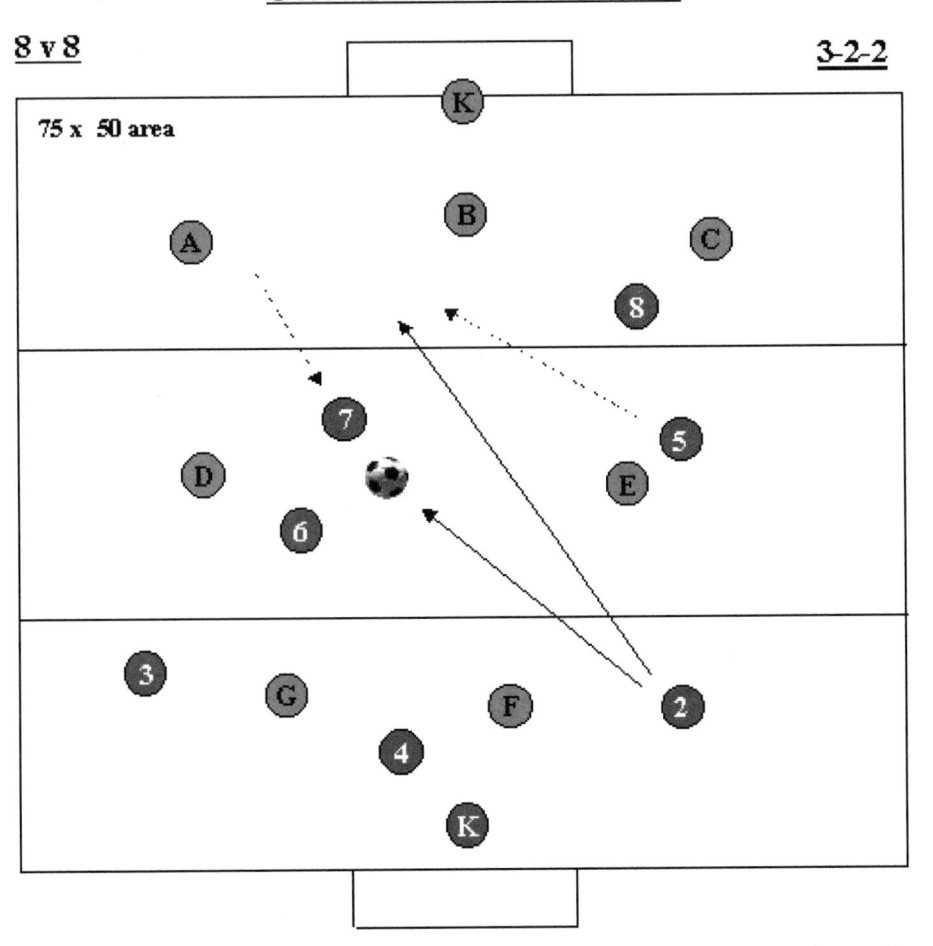

1. **Develop** - Have players able to transition back into zones from the attacking third to the midfield third, the midfield third to the defensive third. Defenders still cannot move between zones.

2. An example could be a striker moves back into the midfield third (to receive to feet or free space for someone else to move into) and a midfielder moves forward into the attacking third.

3. **Develop** - Allow defending players to track attacking players into the other zones. When this happens the above situation means the defender follows the striker going short, creating space behind for another striker to move into or a midfielder to break forward into.

4. Ultimately open the game up so the players have no boundaries to use for focus and see if they can work out how to keep that balance and shape on an open field of play.

ANTICIPATION, IMAGINATION, AWARENESS

TRANSITIONS BETWEEN THIRDS FOR DEFENDERS ALSO

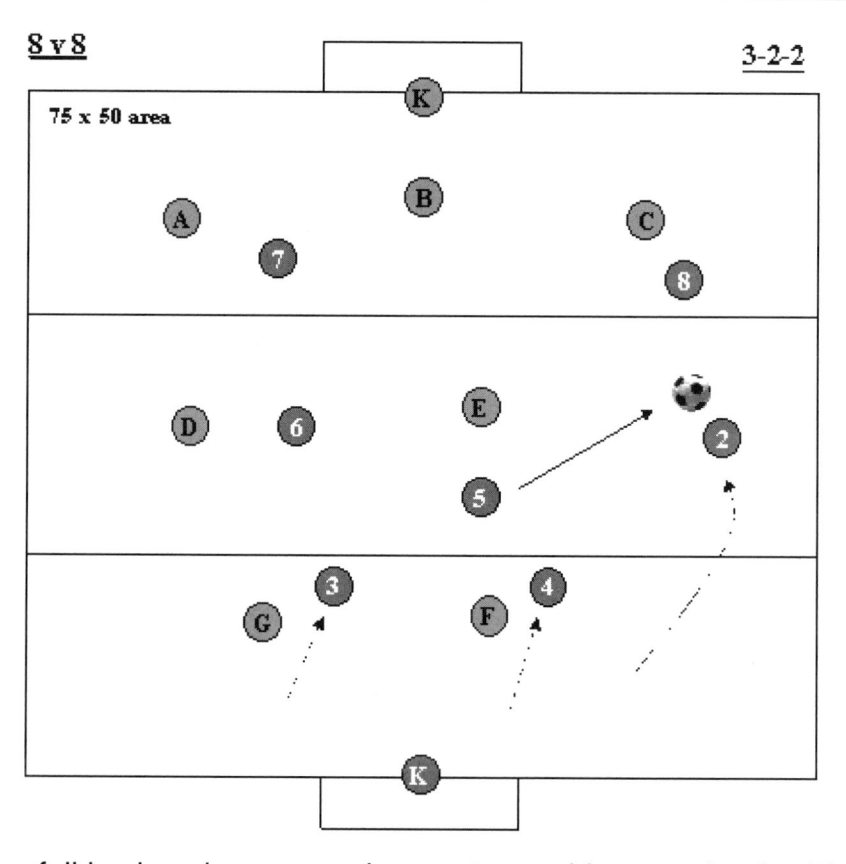

1. Here a full back makes an overlap run to provide an option for (5) to pass to. This is a particular movement that can be practiced and developed in this set up, as the run is difficult for the opposition to identify and counter.

2. The overlap can occur also from the middle third into the attacking third.

3. Playing offside means that the other defenders move up to the edge of the offside line to leave the strikers offside as (2) takes the ball forward.

4. Wide defenders need to be constantly encouraged to get into good wide receiving positions to take the ball forward into attacking areas of the field.

PROGRESSIONAL DEVELOPMENT FROM START TO FINISH

1. Set up is as follows; the field is arranged in thirds; defending, midfield and attacking. In the set up here we have a 3 v 2, a 2 v 2 and a 3 v 2. If you have problems getting the movement going from the back in a 3 v 2 then have a 3 v 1 at each end to begin (to make it easier to find space) and have a 3 v 3 in the middle.

2. STAY IN OWN THIRD.

Players stay in their own thirds to get a feel for how to maintain shape and how to use width in attack. Spread out in possession in a 3 v 2 overload at the back in the defending third to create a situation where the players are available to receive the ball in space and pass it forward.

3. TRANSITON BETWEEN THIRDS

Players are allowed to transition between thirds but only one at a time. The defending team cannot move between thirds to track the attacking players. When the attacking team loses possession they then become defenders and must immediately drop back into the third they started in. The reason for dropping back and not trying to win it back there and then is because we are working on offensive play and want both teams to have the opportunity to build up play. Players can run the ball in, pass it in, or pass it in to a runner from your own third.

4. TRANSITION OVER TWO THIRDS

Still transitions between thirds but allow players to transition forward over two of the thirds. For example, a defender moves forward into the middle third and ends up in the attacking third. If the move breaks down and the players have to get back into their original shape, have the players identify who needs to drop into the defending third. It may not be the actual defender himself but may be the closest player to the defensive third who can drop back in and cover for them, thus saving a long run back for the defender. Players get back into their correct position when the situation allows. Look for overlap runs from behind the ball.

5. TRANSITION BACKWARDS BETWEEN THIRDS

Allow players to transition between thirds, coming back as the initial movement. For example, a striker may drop back into the middle third to receive. A midfielder may push on into the space the striker created.

6. SWITCHING PLAYERS

Work on movement of midfielders and strikers in terms of play not always being in straight lines. For example, movement across the field where two midfielders may switch positions or up front where strikers can switch about to move defenders around.

7. TRANSITIONS OF DEFENDING PLAYERS

Allow defenders to track players into the other thirds they venture into. Now all players can move between thirds but still only one at a time. This helps highlight how to create space for someone else by the movement of players; a striker comes short, pulls a defender with him and space is created in the area he came from for another striker or a midfielder to move into to receive the pass.

8. OFFSIDE FROM THE DEFENDING THIRD

Introduce offside in the final thirds at both ends of the field. This encourages teams to move up as the ball is played forward.

9. FREE PLAY

Open the game up. See if players can maintain their shape without the help of the thirds, maintaining team balance while transitioning.

10. NUMBER OF TOUCHES RESTRICTION

Introduce a three, two, then one-touch restriction to see if the players can work more quickly and still have success. This speeds up decision making in the game. When it is one touch, condition it so they can take more than one touch (a pass may be so heavy they need two touches) but emphasize the use of one touch if it is on to do so. This keeps it realistic.

11. I would recommend using this session on a regular basis and set it up for the scrimmage you usually do at the end of a coaching session.

ANTICIPATION, IMAGINATION, AWARENESS

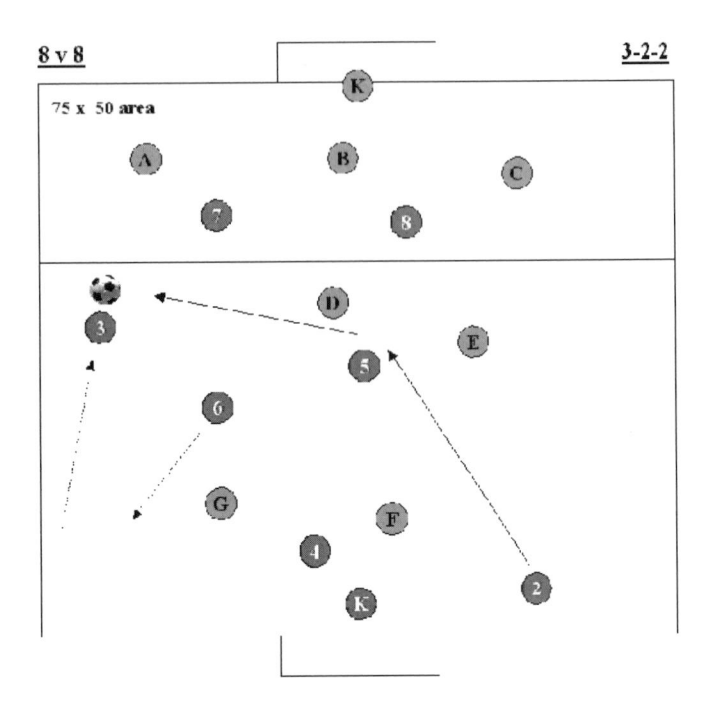

1. Player (2) passes the ball into the middle zone to (5). (3) moves up from the defensive zone to the middle zone to support. This type of transition movement is important because it allows players to move freely between the zones knowing they will have a teammate covering for them.

2. **Develop** - Play offside from the defensive third of the field, encouraging pressing up.

3. In terms of the opposition, this rapid movement and transition makes it difficult for them to pick players up, to read what your team is doing and how it is playing. Usually (D) would be marking (6), but now has to think about marking (3).

4. This means defenders aren't just defenders, midfielders aren't just midfielders and attackers aren't just attackers. They work to help each other through the three units of the team and are free to mix the game up. This is total soccer, played to encourage the free movement of players throughout the teams.

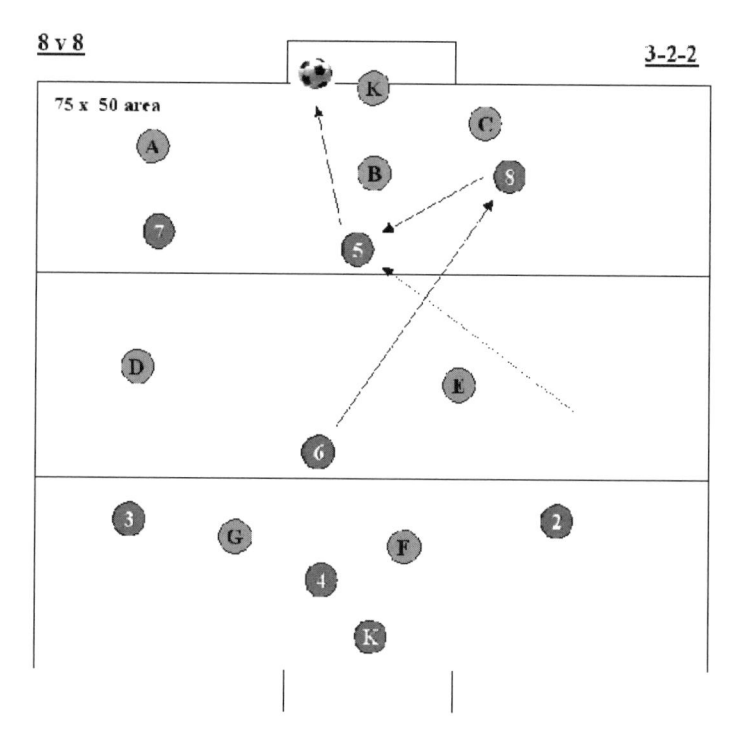

1. Here (6) plays the ball to (8) and (5) makes a run off the ball to support in the attacking third. (8) may be able to lay the ball off for (5) to shoot at goal.

2. You can practice this session with different numbers of players to get the same effect, building up to an 11-v 11 games.

3. Transitions can depend on the stage of the game; if your team is a goal down, (7) would probably stay in the attacking third, not cover for (5) to keep an overload situation there. But the basis of the session is to show how to maintain a balanced shape in your team.

Develop - Allow defending players to track attacking players into the other zones. Ultimately open the game up so the players have no boundaries to use for focus and see if they can work out how to keep that balance and shape on an open field of play.

TRANSITION FROM
DEFENSIVE TO ATTACKING FORMATION

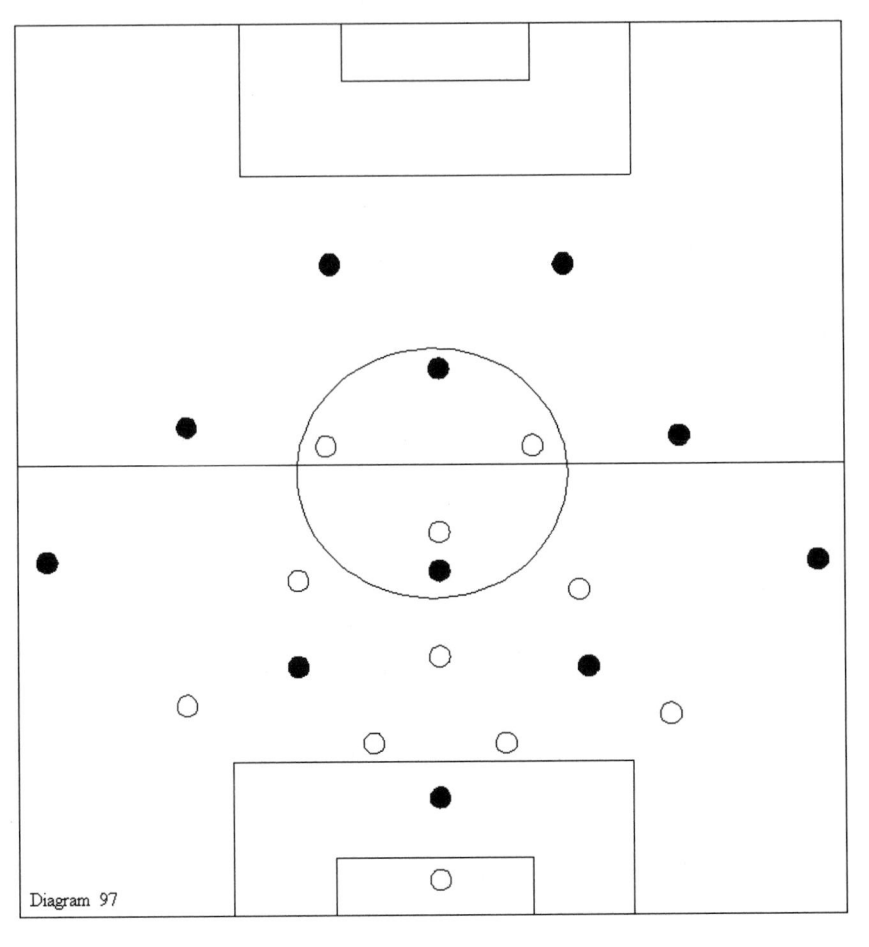

Diagram 97

○ Defending formation - Basic set up, team moves as the ball moves.
● Attacking formation - Basic set up, team moves as the ball moves.

Here is an example of a 4 - 3 - 1 - 2 system of play. You can set this up with your preferred system to achieve the same results. The principles are the same: creating space on the field using width and length when moving to the attacking set-up.

Note: I am only scratching the surface of how to implement the ideas of this book into the 11 v 11 situations. I plan to delve deeper into this aspect in my next book.

ANTICIPATION, IMAGINATION, AWARENESS

TRANSITION FROM DEFENSE TO ATTACK IN AN 11 V 11

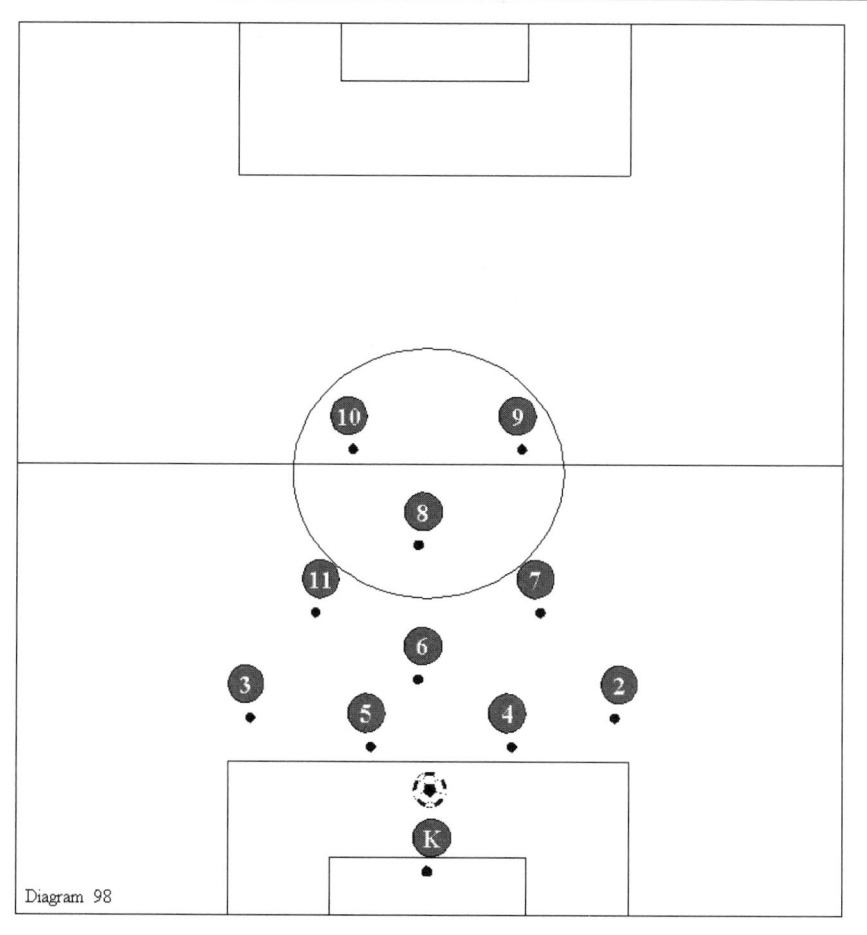

Diagram 98

1. Cone two areas out using different colors to represent **defensive mode** and **attacking mode** (see next page) so players have a focal point to work from. No ball is used to begin. Players move on command between defending and attacking positions until they are comfortable with the movement.

2. Introduce a ball, served from the keeper. Coach calls "attacking mode" and they spread out.

3. When defending, the formula is to **condense** the areas around the ball, filling spaces to make it difficult for teams to play through.

TRANSITION FROM DEFENSE TO ATTACK IN AN 11 V 11

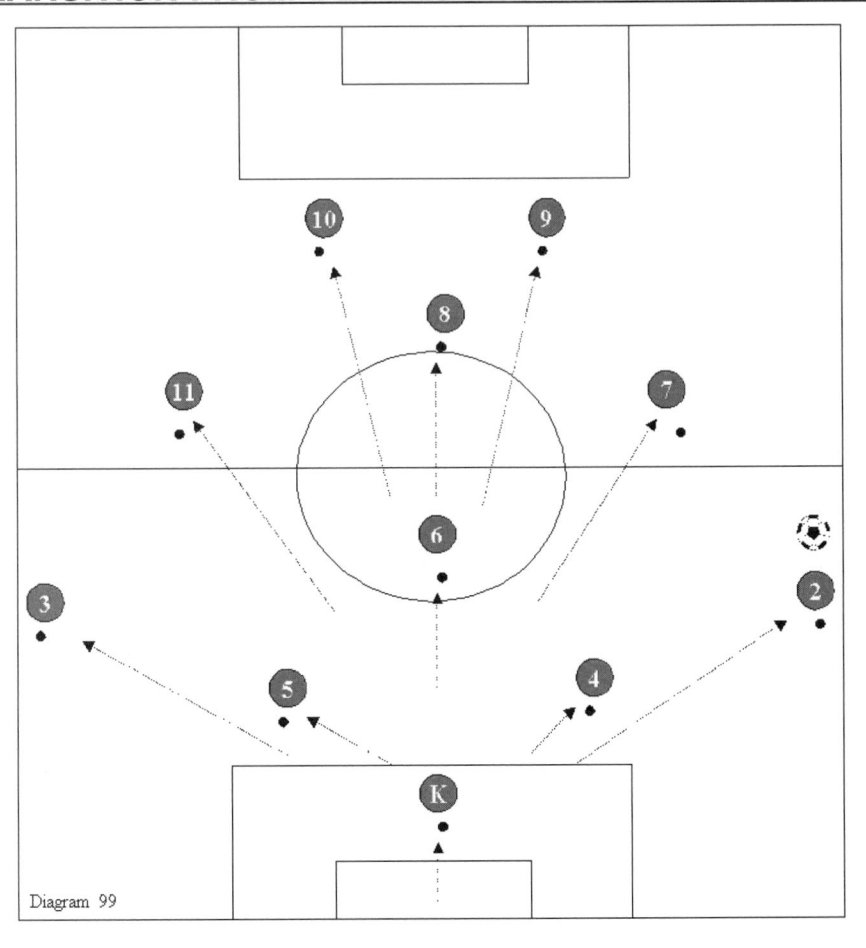

Diagram 99

1. Players have **spread out** into attacking positions to make it difficult for the opposition to mark them. **Shadow play** can be worked now with the ball being delivered generally to a full back in a wide area to attack. Work passing play from here.

2. If you have two teams, **both** can line up as an eleven with the team who receives the ball becoming the attacking team and the other team becoming the passive defensive team.

3. Practice moving from defensive to attacking team shape quickly. Once the ball has been passed down one side, the team shifts across closer to the ball (distances depend on ages of players). Younger players mean shorter distances between the players as they can't pass the ball as far, but the basic shape remains the same.

TRANSITION FROM DEFENSE TO ATTACK IN AN 11 V 11

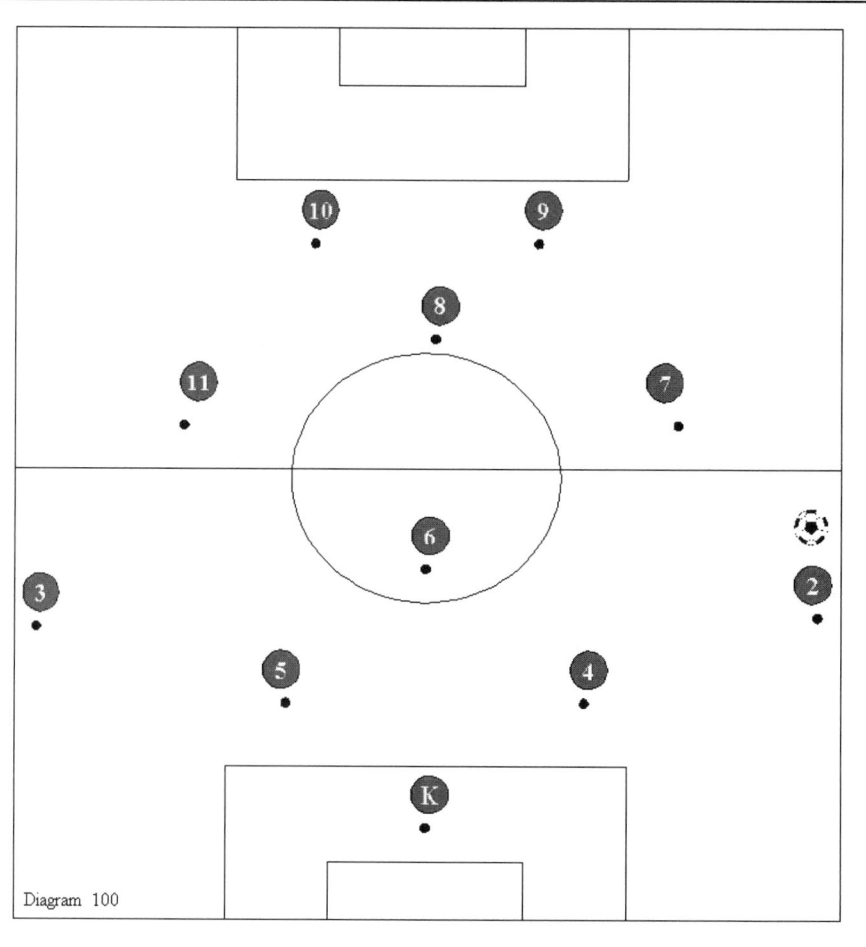

Diagram 100

1. Here we are working with a **4-3-1-2** system, essentially a **diamond** in midfield with a defensive midfielder and an attacking midfielder and two side midfielders who can break wide to support the wide defenders when they attack from the back.

2. Looking to play **high up** the field as a team, using a **high-pressure** method of play but having the capacity to play low pressure when needed. The team is organized to change into a more **defensive set up** for example, when the opposition are having a strong attacking spell. We do this by dropping back player (6) to sweeper, and (8) to defensive central midfield and changing shape to a **5-3-2**.

3. To go full high pressure as a team, we simply push (8) forward in front of the two strikers (4-3-3) and onto the opponents sweeper if they use one.

PLAYING WITH AN EXTRA STRIKER IN A 4-3-3 SYSTEM

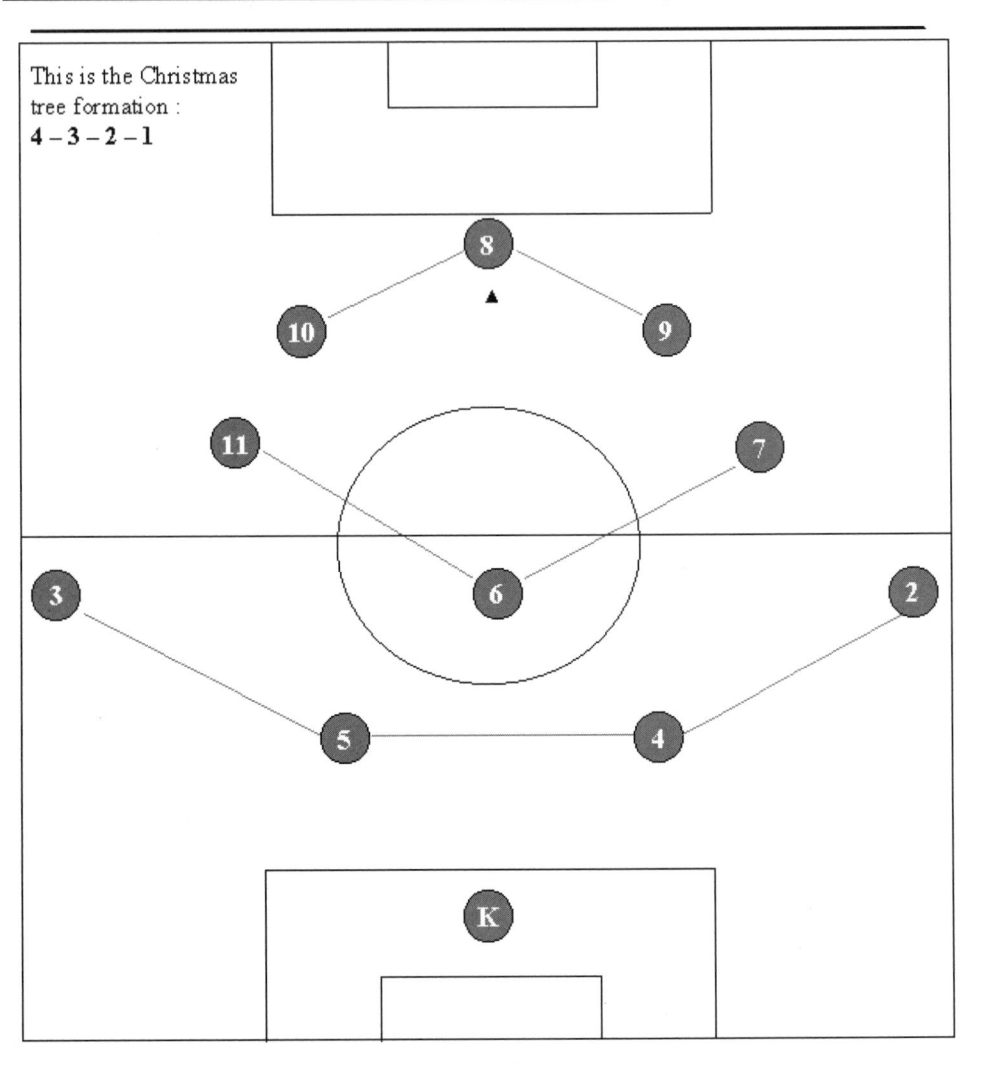

This is the Christmas tree formation :
4 – 3 – 2 – 1

This shows how the attacking midfielder pushes onto the opponent's sweeper (if they play with one) and we go 3 v 3 up front, leaving the opposition with two choices; to stay with no cover or to change their shape to give cover. This way we can implement a full high - pressure situation more easily.

DEFENSIVE SHAPE WHEN UNDER PRESSURE (5-3-2)

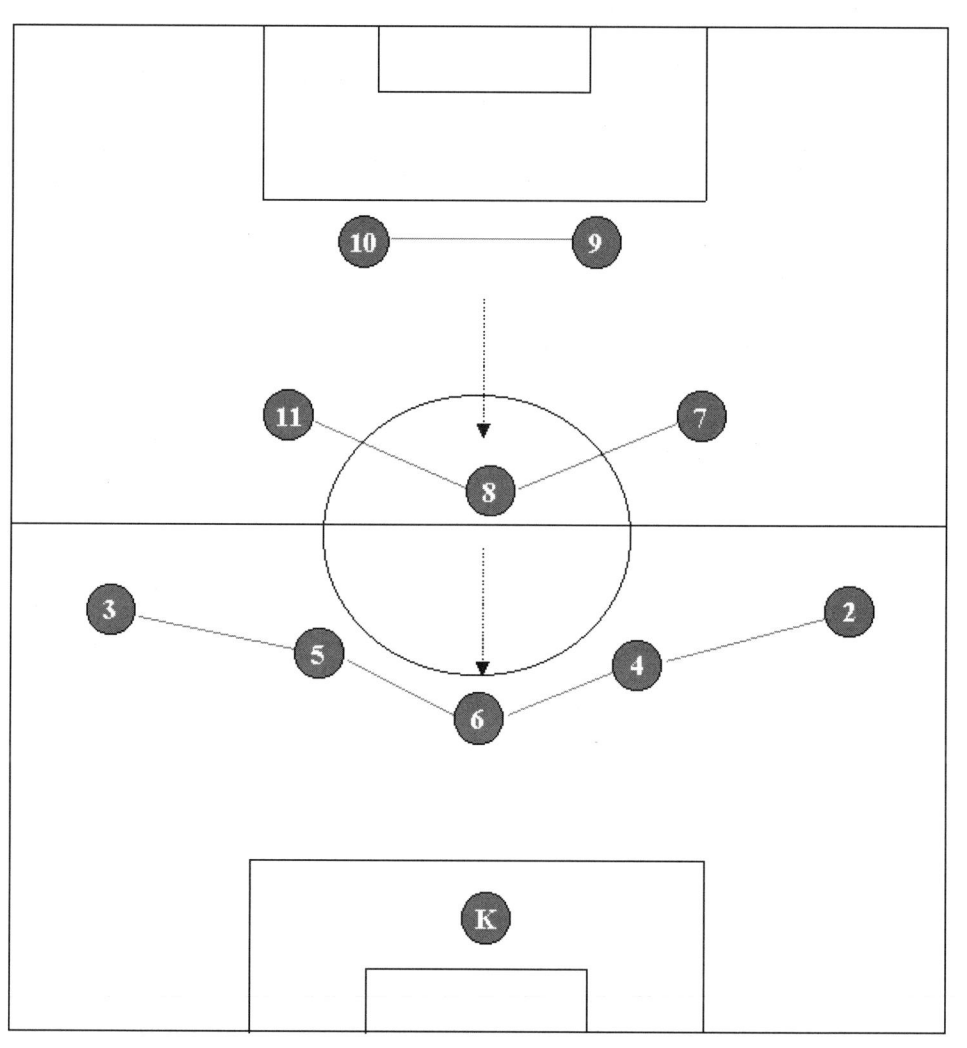

Here we defend with a lower pressure set up where the defensive mid-fielder drops back to sweeper and the attacking midfielder drops back to the defensive midfield position.

Hence we have five players at the back to provide extra cover.

SHADOW TRAINING SESSION
TO PRACTICE TEAM SHAPE

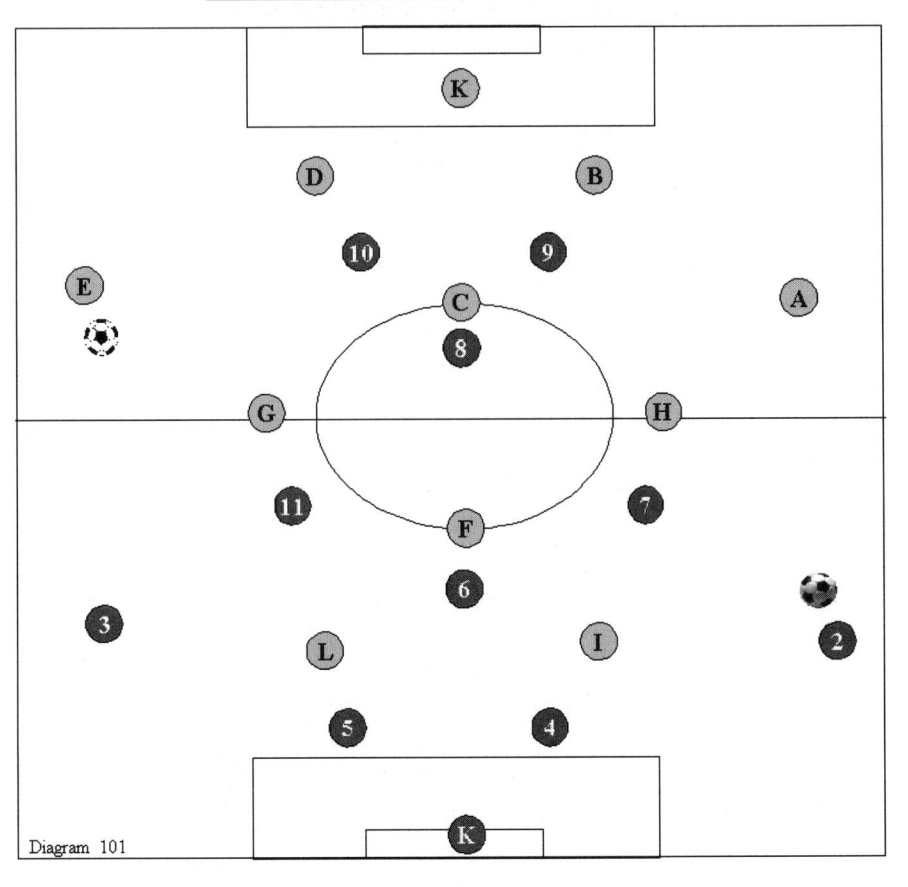

Diagram 101

1. Two teams with a ball each. Each team uses the other team as opposition in the sense that they fill the spaces on the field so they have to play **through** each other, but they aren't playing against each other.

2. This is a **Shadow play** exercise to help each team understand the system of play and be able to practice it freely **without** losing the ball. Begin with one team only passing and moving the ball up the field and taking up the appropriate positions depending on the position of the ball. Once they can understand that, introduce the other team who has also practiced alone first. Once they are comfortable with this, go into a game situation. As a coaching session you can progress it this way and make coaching points during the game situation.

3. I have included 11 v 11 situations in a small way just to show how the A.I.A method of coaching can be developed up to the full game work out. Within the team concept, players are still applying the theme of "looking before receiving", but now it is on the big stage with more variables to consider. This is when each player's A.I.A. capacity is most tested and it is the ultimate situation within which you as the coach can identify what level of awareness each player has reached by their actions on the field.

CONCLUSION AND DISCUSSION

The theme running through all these practices is quite simply teaching the players to LOOK BEFORE THEY RECEIVE THE BALL, to identify in advance all the options they have in front of them depending on where their teammates and the opposition players are positioned. This is the raw ingredient we are trying to establish in the players' minds above all else. All the other aspects related to this requirement fall into place as you go through the program. Everything I am attempting to show you in this book stems from this simple basic philosophy.

I hope this has given you some insight into the thought processes that a player must go through in order to assimilate all that goes with playing soccer successfully.

It must be clear that this isn't a book that covers many different topics but is focused on the basic fundamentals of performance in soccer and to enable the players to have a preparation standpoint from which future development of their game can take place. It hasn't been my intention to cover the technique of shooting or heading but to develop the link between the mind and the body in terms of the development of soccer players.

Most of the work is small sided game activity where the players get lots of touches on the ball and are able to get concentrated practice of the fundamentals they need to learn. The majority of the exercises have the players spending considerable time touching and manipulating the ball and it is advisable that the coaches allow this to happen. Don't spend too much time explaining and thus stopping the momentum of the exercises. Show the players what you want, then let them get on with it, stepping in to make coaching points where and when it is appropriate.

Where you can use small sided groups, do so. If you have a squad of twenty players, for example, it is best to split them in two and have each group perform the exercise in question. Numbers don't always allow for the best way to develop any particular exercise but it is up to the individual coach to use his / her imagination and experience to set it up to allow the players to use the exercise in the best way possible. Always include a soccer ball or several soccer balls in the exercises so players always have the opportunity to practice their skills.

This book has been a journey of discovery for me, as I hope it has been for you the reader in it's content and focus. It is a different approach that I have taken from conventional soccer coaching books but one that I think is important to explore in terms of the requirements needed to become a soccer player.

The coach can develop from this book (with a little imagination) new ideas on how to progress his / her players on the principles of the A.I.A. program. I do not have the exclusive rights of thought on this. I want this book to be the catalyst to encourage coaches to aid the further development of coaching by producing their own ideas and views on the topic and helping to take it's development even further.

This is the beauty of the game, people embracing an idea and improving it's content, it's effectiveness, being inspired to take it to the next level. Have the confidence to read it, use it, break it down and change it to suit your own needs and those of your players. Value your own perspective and use this insight to help your players become the best they can and in turn you will be on the road to be the best you can be as a coach.

On reading this book and using it's methods of coaching, if you believe it has helped you become a better coach, helped your understanding of the thought processes a player has to go through and ultimately guided you into producing better players (which is why we all do it), then I have achieved my goal.

Thank you for taking the time to share with me the love and enthusiasm I have for this wonderful game. We never stop learning and improving our knowledge and must strive to be the best we can be. We owe this not just to ourselves, but more importantly to all the players we coach over the years.

E-mail: wayneharrison-epsc@mn.rr.com
Website: waynesworld-of-soccer.com

Also available from Reedswain:

#149 **Soccer Tactics**
by Massimo Lucchesi
$12.95

#243 **Coaching Team Shape**
by Emilio Cecchini
$12.95

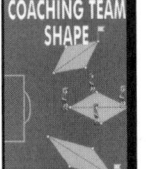

#249 **Coaching the 3-4-3**
by Massimo Lucchesi
$12.95

#256 **The Creative Dribbler**
by Peter Schreiner
$14.95

#265 **Coordination, Agility and Speed Training for Soccer**
by Peter Schreiner
$14.95

#794 **248 Drills for Attacking Soccer**
by Alessandro del Freo
$14.95

#905 **Soccer Strategies**
by Robyn Jones and Tom Tranter
$12.95

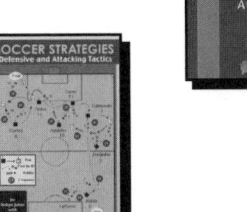

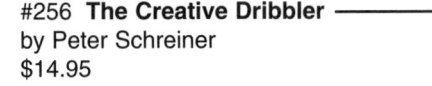

www.reedswain.com
800.331.5191